Praise fo

"My heart sings as I read Bob's words. In this book he takes us beyond facile or formulaic articulations of the Christian life in which our performance always seems to slip in as the key ingredient to calm and joy. Instead Bob plunges our hearts into the deep and wondrous truths of the biblical gospel where Jesus and his grace for ongoing sinners is so real that our cynicism and hardness and discouragement don't stand a chance! Thank you for helping me to repent, believe, and fight, Bob!"

Dane Ortlund, author of *Gentle and Lowly* and Pastor of Naperville Presbyterian Church

"As the herald of God's grace in Christ (1 Tim 2:7; 2 Tim 1:11), the apostle Paul would warmly endorse, I believe, this enticing invitation to participate in what Dr. Flayhart creatively calls the Gospel Waltz."

Murray J. Harris, Professor Emeritus of New Testament Exegesis and Theology at Trinity Evangelical Divinity School in Deerfield, Illinois, and one of the original NIV translators

"I hope that Bob Flayhart's pastoral thoughts on gospel transformation receive a wide reading in the church."

Bryan Chapell, Pastor Emeritus of Grace Presbyterian Church in Peoria, Illinois and President Emeritus of Covenant Theological Seminary in St. Louis, Missouri

"*The Gospel Waltz* is a thoughtful and insightful book inviting us all to join the Father in the ancient dance of life and faith and love. Thank you, Bob, for encouraging us to listen intently to the rhythm of His grace and join in His great round dance of love."

Jim Branch, Director of Core Leadership in Knoxville, Tennessee and author of *The Blue Book: A Devotional Guide for Every Season of Your Life*

"I am so moved and stirred by your words of encouragement. Your words strengthen my hope in Jesus and help fuel my faith in Jesus moving forward. I truly hope this book will be a huge help to others and take some teaching load off of counselors and those who are being used by God to point people to our hope in the gospel. Weekly in the counseling office I hear a new client say, 'I've never heard the gospel explained that way, and I've been in an evangelical church for thirty years. How can this be? Am I even a believer?' Our ministry will purchase a case load of your books to distribute to our clients. *The Gospel Waltz* takes a lot of the teaching work off of us!"

Julie Sparkman, professional counselor

"During forty years in ministry, I've met countless church-goers who profess faith in Jesus and articulate sound doctrine but who have not been transformed by it. They have never experienced the power of the gospel; they don't know the kiss of the Father. Bob Flayhart's *The Gospel Waltz* aims to remedy this. Bob is a master instructor in the footsteps of God's grace, and this wise book will soon have you dancing with gospel joy."

Ray Cortese, church planter and pastor for 40 years at Seven Rivers Church, Lecanto, Florida

The Gospel Waltz

The Gospel Waltz

Experiencing the Transformational Power of Grace

Bob Flayhart
with Holly Mackle

GCD Books

The Gospel Waltz: Experiencing the Transformational Power of Grace

GCD Books
Austin, TX

GCD Books is a ministry of Gospel-Centered Discipleship. Our purpose is to produce resources that make, mature, and multiply disciples of Jesus.

To get more resources from Gospel-Centered Discipleship, visit us at GCDiscipleship.com/books and follow us on Twitter @GCDiscipleship.

GCD editorial: Lauren Bowerman, Lainee Oliver
Front cover design: Laura Schembre (copperstreetdesign.com)
Back cover & interior design: Benjamin Vrbicek

Paperback ISBN: 978-1-73-674469-7
Ebook ISBN: 979-8-98-892980-2

Contents

For Laurie: All these years . . .
and still you open my eyes to grace

INTRODUCTION

As soon as my granddaughter, Harmony, was adopted by my son Josh and my daughter-in-law Kara, they noticed how much she loved music. She often responded to it by dancing on her chubby, nearly-two-year-old legs, spinning around in circles until she dropped over dizzy. From Motown to Disney princess anthems, from classical instrumentations to "Baby Shark," Harmony loves music, and she loves to dance.

One day I put on a song from the animated movie *Tangled*, and Harmony started her circles, inviting me to join her. I am not much for getting dizzy, so after a moment I grabbed her hands and integrated her circles with the disco twist. We were swaying joyfully back and forth to all things princess when suddenly Harmony dropped my hands and raised her arms as if to say, *Pick me up. Hold me. Dance with me.* How could I say no? I held her close, spinning her in circles, her eyes locked on mine. As she relaxed into me I imagined my son at her wedding, holding her close for the father-daughter dance. After a few moments I figured she'd had enough, so I put her down. But she immediately lifted her hands back up, and we began to dance again—back and forth, swaying and spinning, motioning to the music with joyful abandon until the song was through.

I confess I thought nothing of our dancing session until I saw the video my wife had recorded from her quiet post in the doorway. Seconds into watching the video my eyes brimmed with tears. Harmony was opening her life to mine. She was asking for a relationship, for rest, for shared joy . . . and she was inviting me to be one of the ones to join her.

Harmony does not understand adoption yet. She does not understand "forever family" or the sacrifice of self her birth mother made to carry her to full term. But she understands I am her "Baba" (my given grandfather name), and she understands that I want to dance with her.

I feel so privileged to have this little girl in my life, and I am not even her daddy (just her daddy's daddy). But that day, and every day since, everything in me has wanted to give her a sense of security, love, acceptance, and safety. If all these longings could ever be fulfilled in a moment, it was in that moment of dancing with Harmony. If those longings rushed so readily from my limited and imperfect heart, how much more must our perfect and all-loving Father desire those things for me—for us!

What has Harmony been delivered from? I may never fully know. But I know the family she has been delivered to. It's a family where she has not only a mom and dad who are filled with excitement and love and the longing to be godly parents, but also an extended family who cannot imagine themselves without her. In addition, she has a Christian community who is committed to do all they can to love her in the covenant family of God.

If you are a believer in Jesus, you are Harmony. We are all Harmony. Like her, we long for relationship and rest. Like her, we long for the accepting embrace of our Father. And like her, we may not understand much. Sometimes we are dancing cluelessly along while the Father is filled with longings for us to experience his immeasurable grace, love, mercy, kindness, and goodness. As he holds us he feels all of that in an instant, and when we catch even a glimpse of it, we are overwhelmed.

Many more dances with Harmony have followed, and hopefully many more await us in the days to come. But during that one dance with her, I learned so much about the Father's heart toward me as his child. In fact, I experienced more of the doctrines of grace, justification, and adoption than I have learned in years of study and preaching. Colossians 1:13 tells us, "He has delivered us from the domain of darkness and transferred us to the kingdom of his beloved Son." We have been transferred from the kingdom of darkness to the kingdom of light. Yet until our total and complete delivery to our long-awaited eternal home, we are being invited to dance today, in the here and now, dipping and swaying and spinning as he "turns [our] mourning into dancing" (Ps. 30:11). This book is about us being invited to experience the joyful abandon that I call waltzing with Jesus—the three step dance with Christ toward transformation that is Repent, Believe, Fight. We are being invited to dance with the One who plays music to our souls.

1

TO THE CHRISTIAN LONGING FOR CHANGE

The Try-Harder Mentality

When I was first converted, I was initiated into a paradigm of spirituality that said if I was to grow in my faith I needed to read my Bible more, pray more, share my faith more, get involved in more Bible studies, worship more, give more, and go to church more. You do not have to be an English major to realize the operative word here: more, more, *more*. Now, there is nothing wrong with any of those spiritual activities in and of themselves, but there is plenty wrong with any of those activities as a means to gain or maintain God's love. Those disciplines are actually very important to the Christian life. But for me, the disciplines alone were all I ever heard. As a result, I began to be as performance-oriented in my relationship with God as I was in the rest of my life. I began to see God as a cosmic, demanding killjoy and a hard-driving father. No matter how much I read the Bible, I was not reading the Bible enough. No matter how much I was praying, I was not praying enough. No matter how much I was sharing my faith, I was not sharing my faith enough. Simply put, I was on a treadmill, and I was getting nowhere fast. I was living by the mantra "I think I can," but the reality was more like the end of Shel Silverstein's satirical presentation of the children's story, *The Little Engine that Could:*

> He would not stop as he neared the top!
> And strong and proud he cried out loud,
> "I think I can, I think I can, I think I can!"
> He was almost there when—CRASH! SMASH!
> BASH!
> He slid down and mashed into engine hash . . .
> Which goes to show if the track is tough and
> the hill is rough,
> THINKING you can just ain't enough![1]

Experientially, I found dead ends at every turn. I could not win. When I did seem to succeed, my end was self-righteousness and even more self-sufficiency. And when I failed, the end was self-despair and the need to try even harder. It did not take long for discouragement and exhaustion to hit. Soon I wanted to chuck the faith entirely.

When I have the opportunity to counsel a discouraged Christian, it often becomes apparent that their discouragement commonly stems not from what they are doing, but from what they are not doing. Every one of us seems to be searching for a *dance partner* that will get us to the ball of transformation, and we may not even be aware of it. For discouraged Christians, it may be that they are dancing with even the good things of the Christian life—mercy, justice, discipleship, evangelism, righteousness, and more. But even the good

---

[1] Shel Silverstein, *Where the Sidewalk Ends* (New York: Harper Collins Publishers, 1974), 158.

things in and of themselves will not lead or even partner you toward transformation. Though they are good, they are insufficient. Though they are good, they fall short of the "best thing," which is Christ himself. As one of my mentors and friends, Bryan Chapell, has often said, many Christians are not wrong in what they say, but in what they leave unsaid. All the good things of the Christian life are indeed good things, but ultimately they are not the source of change. The good things are not an end in themselves, but various means to The End, and The End is Christ (Rom. 10:4; Col. 1:15–21). If we fail to remind ourselves of this, the good *things* in life will overtake the good *Shepherd* in life. And the result will be disastrous.

It is when we attempt to make these good things our end goal that discouragement takes root. And the root of discouragement is invariably pride—either on the try-harder side of the ditch (believing I am capable of getting it right) or on the give-up-before-I've-begun side (believing I *should* be able to get it right but never will). Any partner other than Jesus himself will lead us in all the wrong steps and guide us in an offbeat rhythm, steering us into a ditch of defeat. But as soon as we embrace Jesus—for the entire Christian life from start to finish—we are enabled to step into all the arenas of life to which we are called (Col. 2:6). We are able to keep them in their proper place while Christ is exalted in his.

The Measuring Stick Mentality

Not all fall into the try-harder ditch as I tend to do. Believers who are more tender to seeing their sin (or even obsessing over it) are more likely to perceive others as having it more together than they. This mentality can quickly lead a believer to slip into self-despair as they regularly pull out the measuring stick and mark themselves short. Sadly, the Christian who is more tender to realizing they do not measure up is still in the paradigm of performance because while they recognize their failure more quickly, they often do not see any way out of the despair they are experiencing. They know they cannot pull themselves up by their own bootstraps, but at the same time they do not have any confidence that they are able to live the Spirit-filled life.

It's like J. R. R. Tolkien's Frodo who, after bearing the weight of the ring for some time, told his best friend, "Sam, I just can't do this anymore." The Christian with a self-despairing tendency knows the metaphorical bootstraps of the try-harder life will not hold. At times, this keeps them from even attempting to do much of anything at all in their pursuit of gospel holiness. But their entire premise is wrong, because ultimately it is not about them "doing it." It is about what the Spirit can do, so the foundation of their despair is still living in the paradigm of self-reliance. While the more sensitive Christian often falls into discouragement or despair first—even years before the self-reliant and disciplined Bootstraps Theology practitioner—it is the latter who may fall more deeply into the pit of self-despair when they finally realize their self-reliance just cannot produce the holiness God requires.

Satan's Greatest Tool

For both types of believers, the realities of daily living hardly sound like the promises of the joyful Christian life. Whether someone struggles with the "Try Harder" mentality or wrestles with the "Measuring Stick" mentality, they often ask themselves, "Is this all there is?" Both commonly face the doldrums of defeat and the frustrations of failure in the Christian life after salvation. In fact, early in my Christian life I had a season of thinking that I had been much happier as an unbeliever than I was as a Christ-follower. Knowing I would go to heaven when I died just did not seem to be enough. What about any kind of joy and peace and victory *now*? How does one rejoice when life can seem more messed up as a Christian than it was as a non-Christian? What does a Christian do with downright discouragement?

Perhaps you have heard the story of the devil getting ready to sell some of his tools and laying them all out on a table. Envy, greed, hatred, anger, bitterness, lust, impatience—they are all there, priced and ready for sale. Off to the side, there is what appears to be a very unimpressive tool, and yet next to it is a sign that says "not for sale." Some of the young apprentice demons run up to Satan and ask, "Why is this one not for sale?" Satan replies, "You know, most Christians are pretty guarded against many of the tools I have, but this one seems to work so easily. If I use this tool on them, it opens their hearts for any other tool I want to use. And that is why it will never be for sale." What is Satan's subtle tool to open our hearts to any other temptation he wants to throw at us? *Discouragement.*

When Christians are discouraged, we are more susceptible to temptation and sin than at any other time in our lives. Why? Consider the inevitable progression when we are discouraged. We experience deep or unexpected pain. Pain sets us on a quest for relief to take the edge off, and in this discouragement predicament Christians sometimes turn to many of the same sins and excesses as the world to self-medicate. Much like those who do not follow Jesus, we look for something to dull the painful ache in our souls, and so we turn to the same coping mechanisms, typically represented by something in excess: alcohol, Netflix, work, food, exercise, planning, shopping . . . or just plain old immorality.

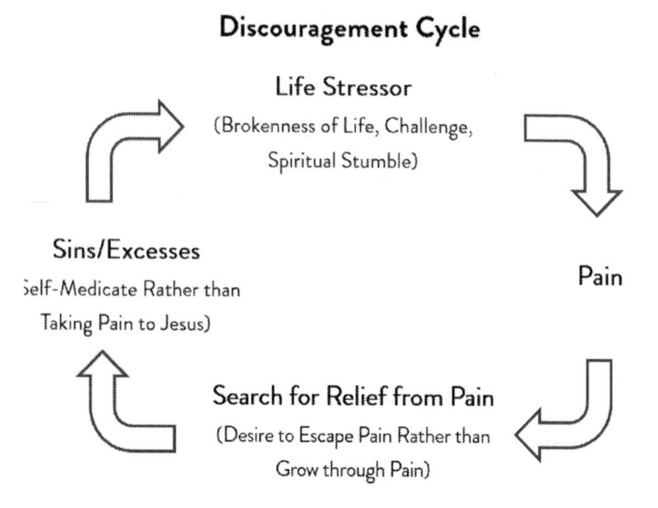

Seeing this discouragement cycle and the false power it holds can actually help us recognize that we are often trying to win a game that has already been won on our behalf. For many, what lies at the root of the discouragement cycle in the Christian life is an inadequate understanding of and lack of true hope in the gospel.

Settle the Fundamentals

When our three children were quite young, I got to help coach all of them in basketball. I loved teaching their young age groups because I love teaching the basics—the fundamentals. *Dribble with only one hand at a time. Once you stop dribbling, you can't start again; you either have to pass or shoot.* Imagine a child who has been taught all the basics. Now imagine their shock, perhaps five years down the road, when they find out for the first time that they had never been taught the key aim of basketball: *You have to get that little ball in that steel hoop in order to score points and win.* It would be a travesty to teach people the basics of basketball but never tell them the objective of the entire game. But I fear, to some extent, that is what has happened in many of our churches and in our Christian lives. We have been taught all kinds of basics—the behaviors. We have been taught all kinds of fundamentals—the disciplines. But have we emphasized the point of the whole Christian life: Jesus himself and hope in our union with him both now and in eternity?

Fundamentals function only if there are agreed upon rules. Take basketball: without the rules of basketball, no one can play. These rules are not tips to get better or to know the game more. Rather, they are boundaries for playing the game so that someone does not heave the ball into the crowd and call it a three-pointer. Without agreed-upon laws, there is no game. In the same way, the true fundamentals of the Christian life—faith and hope in Christ—are impossible to understand without some ground rules. These rules are not behaviors and disciplines that might help us to be more spiritual; they are far more vital and foundational. They are unbending directives given by a loving Shepherd who longs for us to understand grace and to know him intimately. Salvation is by grace from first to last, from beginning to end, from

A-Z. We never move beyond grace, we simply keep moving more deeply into it.

The Fundamentals of Grace

As followers of Christ we must learn to believe that trusting in Christ on a daily, moment-by-moment basis brings about holiness the same way it brought about salvation. Christ lived a perfect life, died a substitutionary death, then sent his Holy Spirit so that we could live in righteousness and holiness. Salvation is a permanent, powerful, and irreversible process begun and continued by the Spirit of God. In response, Ephesians 4:23–24 reminds us to be made new in the attitude of our minds and to put on the new self—created to be like God, in true righteousness and holiness. The work of Christ was not accomplished merely to bring us to heaven. Rather it also renews us today and every day in the depths of our hearts, the attitudes of our minds, the feelings of our souls, the desires of our beings, and the choices of our wills (Matt. 22:37). That is something that is done in us and to us, not out of our own effort, but through faith and trust in the gospel promises.

The work of Christ was not accomplished merely to bring us to heaven. Rather it also renews us today and every day in the depths of our hearts, the attitudes of our minds, the feelings of our souls, the desires of our beings, and the choices of our wills.

As we are renewed in the attitude of our minds, we will find the capacity to rejoice and avoid the discouragement that opens us up so easily to temptation and sin. But what are these promises on which we reflect to remind us of our standing before a holy God? We will gradually flesh out each of these in detail, but before we proceed it is vital to establish the fundamentals that the assertions of the Gospel Waltz will be based on.

- We are justified by faith, not by works. (Rom. 3:28; Gal. 2:16)
- We are adopted children of God. His love for us is not dependent on our record of performance. (Rom. 8:15; Eph. 1:5; John 14:18)
- We still deal with indwelling sin. If we are in Christ, we are brand new—genuinely new—but not yet totally new. (Rom. 7:15–17; Gal. 5:17; 1 Pet. 2:11)
- Though we do possess a new response-ability, we do not possess the ability to heal ourselves from our sin problem, and must therefore be sanctified by grace. We may be able at times to change our behaviors, but we are incapable of changing our own hearts. (Titus 2:11–12; Acts 20:32; Phil. 1:6; 2 Pet. 2:3–4)
- Ultimate renewal, also called glorification, is promised upon Christ's return. (Rom. 8:30)
- God is sovereign. Yet our choices matter. (Phil. 2:12–13)
- There is no secular/sacred dichotomy. The gospel applies to every aspect of our lives. (Col. 1:16, 20)
- The Christian life is supernatural. It is more than a discipline; it is the present power of the gospel and the daily working of the Holy Spirit. (Gal. 3:1–5)
- God is real, his Word is true, he is good, and heaven is sure. (Num. 23:19; Ps. 18:30)

Many of the above are doctrinal concepts that we can study and begin to conceptually grasp in this life until we are able to fully grasp them in heaven. But we will not capture a life-changing grasp on them until we see that they all fall under the same umbrella of God's grace. Grace is not merely a concept or an en vogue word people toss around. Neither is grace something you simply assent to. Grace is a living power; it is the very power of God (Acts 20:32; Rom. 1:16). It is not merely the message of his love. It is the activity of his love. And believing in, hoping in, and resting in this grace is the key to the Christian life. It is so key, in fact, that the Apostle Paul summed up his entire calling by referring to it: "But I do not account my life of any value nor as precious to myself, if only I may finish my course and the ministry that I received from the Lord Jesus, to testify to the gospel of the grace of God" (Acts 20:24).

I am reminded of a friend and mentor, Dr. Paul Kooistra, who, when I was in a season of self-doubt over whether I was overemphasizing grace, shared with me, "Bob, when people ask me why I talk so much about grace, I say, 'Because there is nothing else to talk about.'" I've developed the Gospel Waltz as a tool to help us keep the grace of God at the center of our lives.

Cheap Grace?

Not all receive the invitation to dance the Gospel Waltz with open arms. Right now some of us may feel a little cynicism churning below the surface upon considering this emphasis on God's grace, his unconditional love, his favor, and his blessing upon undeserving sinners in Christ. Remember the story from my conversion—doing more, more, *more*, all in the name of pleasing God? Well, God was merciful to show me the error of my paradigm. He was kind to draw me to repentance and grace, radically rocking my performance mindset. I learned that we all grow best in the fertile soil of grace. But as I began to search the Bible, trying to wrap my arms around grace, people sometimes questioned whether I was leading my church astray or falling into libertinism.

I recall many interactions with one particular friend who assumed that a focus on grace meant a minimization of the concept of obedience or holiness. Ironically it was actually his view of grace that was truncated. He only saw grace as unconditional love, not as transforming power. While he would not have assented to it doctrinally, his arguments revealed his belief that conversion was by grace, but that sanctification was through an entirely different power—our own. No matter how many conversations we had, it seemed like we were always talking past each other. What followed was a very hurtful season of ministry for me. I would often have to remind myself of the assertion of Welsh pastor and author David Martyn Lloyd-Jones—that if your preaching does not open you up to the (inaccurate) accusation of antinomianism (a heresy minimizing the importance of obedience to God's commands) and open you up to the (unjust) charge of preaching a grace that asks nothing in return—then you can be assured you are not preaching the gospel.[2]

---

[2] D. Martyn Lloyd-Jones, *Romans: The New Man. Exposition of Chapter 6* (Edinburgh: Banner of Truth, 1989), 8–9.

The charge that grace will make us soft to obedience is not a new one. After an entire chapter about grace as the free gift of God that gives us peace with him, Paul writes Romans 6:1: "What then shall we say? Are we to continue in sin that grace may abound?" Why would Paul even ask such a question in the context of the letter? It must have been that some people were drawing wrong conclusions from Paul's teaching on grace. Paul corrects their erroneous beliefs with the exclamation, "By no means! How can we who died to sin still live in it?" People were misinterpreting Paul's teaching by concluding that the doctrine of grace meant that it did not matter how Christians lived because the more you sinned, the more grace would increase and cover it. This reduced grace to a concept that could be abused, and it minimized grace as a power that actually supernaturally changed a heart. Grace is open to abuse, but Paul did not stop preaching grace just because it was being abused, and the rest of Romans 6 was the result. Paul did not balance cheap grace with law. Instead he cut cheap grace off at the knees with biblical grace. Preaching, teaching, and discipling from a foundation of God's unmerited favor will always be open to abuse, but that is not a reason to stop emphasizing it, especially when it is a key element to living a holy life.

It is easy for all of us to miss the fact that grace is a supernatural power, not a mere concept or theological premise.

Grace for Believers

Those who fear that an emphasis on grace will fail to inspire and enable holiness miss the fact that the only on-ramp to holiness is grace. Those who have seen the detrimental impact of cheap grace—or those who emphasize a rigorous application of the will to the commands of God to change our lives rather than emphasize the grace of God to change us—must be wary of reducing the gospel to a mere philosophical or theological concept that can be absorbed on a rational level. It is easy for all of us to miss the fact that grace is a supernatural power, not a mere concept or theological premise. I can sympathize with those who find themselves a bit skeptical of preaching that emphasizes grace and wonder whether such an emphasis will lead to license to sin, but this begs the question: does the choice to not sin ever occur apart from grace? In Galatians 3:1–3, Paul asks the Galatians: *How did you get here anyway, to a place of seeking after self-attained holiness? Was it by your own effort or by believing the gospel and the work of the Holy Spirit that you were converted? So do you actually think it is by your own effort you will be changed?* Paul does not mince words, and his intensity must likewise grip our attention:

> O foolish Galatians! Who has bewitched you? It was before your eyes that Jesus Christ was publicly portrayed as crucified. Let me ask you only this: Did you receive the Spirit by works of the law or by hearing with faith? Are you so foolish? Having begun by the Spirit, are you now being perfected by the flesh? (Gal. 3:1–3)

During my "grace awakening," this passage brought me tremendous comfort, as it was really the same answer to two different questions: 1) How do I become a Christian? and 2) How do I grow as a Christian? The answer to both is the same: *by the work of the Spirit through believing the gospel.* This revelation rocked my world—so much so that I would hit my knees in desperation as I persisted in preaching grace not just for the convert, but also for the believer. I begged, *Lord, I need wisdom. I need to hear from You. Am I on the right track?* And each time, without fail, I would be led to a passage that affirmed this was the true gospel. At the time, there were not a lot of books on what is now referred to as the "grace movement," so the old saints became my teachers. God used the works of Martin Luther, John Calvin, the Westminster Divines of the 1640s, Walter Marshall, John Owen, and Archibald Alexander to train me in this fresh understanding of grace. As I looked back in church history, I realized this was what the church had taught all along concerning sanctification. But at some point we lost sight of the true fundamentals of the gospel.

Apply the Fundamentals

The entirety of this book will attempt to flesh out a practical application of grace through the paradigm of the Gospel Waltz. If you find yourself discouraged in the Christian life and wondering if this is all there is until we get to heaven, will you consider accepting the invitation to dance? This invitation is an offering of shared vocabulary; it is a way to interact with other believers and with the Trinity over complex concepts (like grace).

Fred Astaire was, without dispute, one of the top singers, dancers, and actors of his day. But believe it or not, in 1932 when Astaire was starting out, a Hollywood talent agent wrote this about him on his screen test: "Can't act, can't sing, can dance just a little." You may feel much the same about your Christian life. You may not feel all that gifted. You may not feel very spiritual. But the question is: *Will you respond to the Father's invitation to dance? Will you believe that he wants to dance with you even if you don't know how? Are you willing to learn to dance just a little? Can you envision allowing him to teach you his steps and carry you when your feet can't even touch the floor?*

Chapter 1 Summary

- The Gospel Waltz (which we will examine in detail in the following chapters) is a 3-step dance with Christ that leads to transformation by grace. Its steps are repenting of our sin, believing the gospel promises afresh, and fighting against sin and for righteousness in our own hearts.
- The discouragement cycle involves deep or unexpected pain, which sets us on a quest for relief to take the edge off, wherein many of us turn to the same sins and excesses as the world to self-medicate the ache in our souls (i.e., coping mechanisms).
- We will never capture a life-changing grasp of the fundamentals of grace until we experience and understand how they all fall under the same umbrella of God's grace.

Reflection Questions

1. How has Bootstraps Theology wormed its way into your individual Christian life? How and when do you lean toward the more disciplined, "I will never stop trying" type of believer? How and when do you lean toward the more sensitive, "I can never do this?" type of believer? And finally, how and when do you lean toward the "I'm doing fine, thank you very much" follower of Christ?
2. When it comes to the concept of holiness, do you tend to emphasize godly character or mercy and justice? Do you tend to emphasize authenticity in brokenness or disciplining yourself for positive change? What has contributed to your emphasis?

3. Do you tend to be more concerned about "cheap grace" or about legalism? What are some factors that lead to your concern?
4. Which of the *fundamentals* behind the Gospel Waltz do you tend to forget or minimize?

2

WHAT'S THE BIG DEAL ABOUT GRACE?

Like many pastors and church leaders, the two years following the Covid-19 pandemic were difficult and tension-filled years of ministry for me. By God's grace I was able to find contentment in who I am in Christ, but finding contentment in God's redemptive work in and around me in the context of ministry was a whole different story. For months it seemed that no matter what decision I made, it was going to be questioned by half of our congregation, criticized by those outside our church, or viewed as just flat-out wrong. Furthermore, the criticism was not just disagreement with such-and-such decision, but *you* are wrong. The accusations felt intensely personal—and they flew from every side, with the "conservatives" calling me too liberal and the "liberals" calling me too conservative. The constant barrage of attacks made finding joy in my life's calling near impossible. Add to that the divisiveness and general grumpiness among Christians and wider culture in many areas, and I simply found myself in a spot where consistent joy and peace felt out of reach.

I have come to realize that my recent experience mirrors what many Christians experience on a regular basis over their lifetime—where consistent joy and peace are always a bit out of reach. This realization has moved my heart toward empathy for the discouraged and toward a compassion that longs to fight for the hearts of my brothers and sisters in Christ. So many of us want to be skipping with the kind of joy that comes from knowing we are loved by God. We feel we should experience the "You have turned my mourning to dancing" mentality from Psalm 30:11 as reality, but in truth we still have not found what we are looking for. When I encounter a joyless Christian in a pastoral context or in the context of friendship, I first have to remind myself that their current discouragement often betrays a deep longing. We all long for a joyful existence, and we do not have to resign ourselves to a joyless Christian life. But many of us have adopted a skewed idea of what the "joyful Christian life" even looks or feels like. We think this type of relationship always leads to actual dancing and skipping! So before we begin, let's define joy within the context of the Christian life: Christian joy is contentment with who I am in Christ, the purposes of God's redemptive plan in and around me, and his pursuit of my heart through every situation in life.[3]

Christian joy is contentment with who I am in Christ, the purposes of God's redemptive plan in and around me, and his pursuit of my heart through every situation in life.

God is the infinitely happy God.[4] And because of his good nature, God has made the way for us to be

[3] Rejoinder to Jeremiah Burroughs, *The Rare Jewel of Christian Contentment* (Edinburgh: Banner of Truth, 1987), 9.

[4] Piper, *Desiring God* (Portland, OR: Multnomah, 1986), 24.

eternally happy—for our joy to be made complete in Christ. The fruit of the Spirit is joy, therefore the work of the Holy Spirit inside us leads to a joy-filled life. As believers, we know this to be true. So why is it that so few people are experiencing joy in the Christian life? Most people experience it at conversion, but then as Paul says in Galatians 4:15, "What has happened to all your joy?" What about joy in the here and now; what about joy today—in the space you occupy?

Grace theorized offers little comfort. It gives only a hazy understanding of concepts at a rational level, like trying to explain the provision, protection, and love of a good father to a street-orphan. You can tell the orphan that it will be great being part of a family, but that is likely to be abstract and therefore meaningless for them. But when you begin to explain that she will never have to sleep in the cold, wet rain again, and instead will always have a soft bed covered in blankets, comfort begins to become real. Then when you share that she will never need to rummage around for food in a garbage can but will always be able to look forward to three meals a day, often with hot, fresh food, something beyond mere comfort begins to be palpable. But more important than all these material comforts, it is when you tell her that when she falls and scrapes her knee, there will be someone there who will always care and will provide medicine and a Band-Aid to make it feel better—to make *her* feel better—then she will begin to taste what it means to be loved.

We are all prone—even on our best days—to think and act like orphans (Lam. 5:1–5; John 14:18). The previous picture of a new life becoming palpable for the street child is the picture of grace we long for—the kind that lights our hearts with joy. We need grace to be more than a theological word we toss around; we need it to have teeth, to be put in practice and change us in ways that we can see and comprehend so that it means something to us both personally and viscerally. We need to be able to experience grace with all our senses: we need to be able to see it, touch it, taste it, smell it, *and* hear it.

And that is just what God did when he wrapped Jesus in skin and made the invisible God visible. He made the Almighty vulnerable. He allowed the One who holds the world in his hands to be cradled and later killed at the hands of his creation. That kind of grace—the kind that gives everything in unrelenting, undeserved, sacrificial love—changes us. Grace is not content with us remaining the broken, sinful people we are, but instead it lovingly and completely alters us, rebuilds us, and releases us in ways we never could have dreamed.

On the afternoon of Thursday, March 25, 2021, myself, my wife (who happens to be a dog breeder), my mother-in-law, six adult Golden Retrievers, and eight four-week-old Golden Retriever puppies huddled in a basement room while an EF-3 long-track tornado tore through our area and down our street. Moments before, a TV weather team had called out the name of our neighborhood and told us to get to our "safe place" immediately. My wife prayed for anything with breath to be spared. God answered her cry, but our property experienced extensive damage. The devastation was immense. Hundreds of feet of pasture fence were destroyed. Forty-five trees, many nearly 100 feet tall, were splayed like Pick-Up-Sticks around our lawn. My mother-in-law's car was crushed by a tree, and all of our landscaping was destroyed.

Once all living creatures were (graciously) accounted for, what began was an immediate and year-long effort to reconstruct, rebuild, and renovate. Without the love and help of many friends and even strangers, recovery would not have come, or it would have taken far longer. But before the rebuild could even begin, it seemed more destruction first had to occur. Destroyed trees had to be chain-sawed off the house, pieced up, and hauled off, leaving massive stumps that then had to be dug out before the lawn could be regraded. It was an immense undertaking on our farm-like property—replacing fencing, redesigning landscaping, planting new trees . . . the list went on.

A year later the transformation was finally a sight to behold! My wife has always loved Magnolia trees. Before, our property only held pines, but now my wife has multiple magnolias to enjoy. I am a lawn man myself, and with new sod and a sprinkler system, my grass is the greenest on the block. This unexpected deconstruction and reconstruction project has turned out to be the renewal program we could never have dared to dream up. Our property is far more magnificent than anything we had before. Those who helped us in the days following the tornado wept over the brokenness, but now they grow teary-eyed alongside us at the transformation. The mystery of God's providential undoing so that he could allow us to experience renewal is beyond understanding. We feel so loved.

The very same mystery of providence is at work in God's grace of sanctification. Through the storms and brokenness of life—as well as in the delightful, sunny circumstances of life—God is pursuing our hearts in a powerful transformational work of love. We do not know all the ins and outs of how it happens (Col. 1:26–27), but when it is all said and done, we feel lighter, we experience a whole range of color, we see the beauty—and so do others.

Our Dance Partner is always relentlessly pursuing us. But if grace is just the *idea* of unconditional acceptance, we can easily become disinterested and dissatisfied with it, as it holds no power. Rather than taking the hand of God, our Dance Partner, as he continually offers himself to us, we instead shrug it off: "Yes, yes, I've danced with you before, and it was great. But I want something else. You don't dazzle me anymore." Praise God that we do not have to be dazzled by Jesus for him to continually extend his hand and invite us to the dance floor.

What's the Big Deal about Grace?

In the earlier days of what I refer to as my "grace-awakening," I was a young pastor at a new church plant, arms linked with a session of eight elders. Early in my process of tasting and understanding grace, three of the eight elders brought concerns before the session meeting that my teaching on grace was not in accord with Scripture. One of the elders even brought a ten-page complaint. Now, my natural tendency is always toward self-doubt—I never assume the position that everyone else is an idiot and I have this all figured out. So this ten-page complaint ushered in a period of severe self-doubt for me. I wondered if I had grossly misapplied what I was reading in the Bible—a very dangerous position for any pastor, much less a new one.

Yet week after week, day after day, and every single time in an astoundingly supernatural way, God reassured me. He either led me to a piece of writing by Calvin or Luther that confirmed my biblical understanding of grace; or a fellow pastor or friend would make a timely and unexpected phone call of reassurance; or someone new to our church would share how they had been feeling hopeless when the wonder and power and hope of the gospel emphasized through my sermons brought them new life. Even now, these stories persist in the faces I see on a regular basis. One of my current elders was a new visitor at the time, and he and his wife (who knew they were already Christians and had assurance of the faith) shared that they felt they had just been converted.

At every moment of self-doubt, God supernaturally nudged me and reaffirmed that this was his gospel—the one, true gospel—and that I was neither going astray nor leading others astray. After studying the Scriptures and spending time in prayer, discussion, and consideration, the time came for the body of elders to address the complaint. The message to the one who wrote the complaint was that I was clearly preaching the gospel in the context of the history of the reformed faith, and it was time to get on board or resign and move along.

I can understand why many people are afraid of grace. If you really think about it, the gospel of grace *is* scary. Where else in life do we see an example of true benevolence, of someone being willing to go to extraordinary measures with the completely pure motive of just wanting to be in relationship with us, changing us into the best version of ourselves? The answer is of course nowhere, which is part of what makes grace so difficult to accept. We want to work for it—we think we *need* to work for it—and therefore we struggle to accept it. In addition, our experience is that when people are assured of unconditional acceptance, they will often abuse it. The fear is that if God's people are fed a steady diet of grace, they will go off the rails.

Sadly, the tumultuous story of my grace awakening is shared by many in the church, both pastors and lay people alike. In fact, I would say if you are not met with opposition at your own grace awakening, well, you just might not be grasping its magnitude. Grace changes everything. *Everything.* The natural and knee-jerk reaction from many, outside of their own grace awakening, is that if you actually preach and believe grace, you will wind up minimizing holiness. When, in fact, the only hope for an obedient life is to be smothered, drenched, and covered in grace.

A word to those who fear Christians running amok at discovering grace: have there been people who "continued in sin so that grace may abound?" (Rom. 6:1). Of course there have been. Though in the extended passage of Romans 6 Paul is calling out the ridiculousness of this line of thinking, we know experientially that of course there have been people who have abused or misapplied grace. We may even know some of them or have done it ourselves. But we cannot change the teaching of biblical grace just because there are people who abuse it. An unanticipated benefit of biblical grace is that it may actually expose fakes.

I know that at the base of the three elders' concerns about my preaching of grace was fear—fear that people might abuse grace. But perhaps, just maybe, there was also a fear of the mess that would be exposed in our church and in our lives. Where grace is *not* preached, the church is likely just as messy, or perhaps even *more* messy than in a body where grace is preached. But the mess is all underground, blindly ignored, or worse, hidden. The view is that sin is what bad Christians do, so who wants to admit they are bad? So sin remains underground, leaving neat, tidy, clean, seemingly un-messy churches.

But if there is no mess when the Word of God is taught, then real tragedy lurks in the wings. For it means that few are dealing with their real-life messes, because so few are willing to admit to them. People will only be willing to reveal their sin in a safe environment, and likely the safety factor within a church that is not preaching grace is very low. It is likely their attendees focus their concern in the realm of theoretical messes, or large, highly-public behavioral messes. Or perhaps they are overly focused on cultural or political issues outside of themselves, unwilling to deal with the disaster inside their own hearts.

Grace welcomes mess because grace is equipped to deal with it. Therefore grace-filled churches will be messy churches because they prove themselves to be a safe place for transformation.

Grace welcomes mess because grace is equipped to deal with it. Therefore grace-filled churches will be messy churches because they prove themselves to be a safe place for transformation. Churches that do not preach grace are messy too. But, sometimes perhaps the messiness of their hearts is not getting addressed, and therefore the people are not being transformed. You cannot deal with a mess you cannot see.

Looking back, I now view those tumultuous early days of trial and refinement of the message of my pastoral career as a blessing. In his kindness, God allowed me to zero in on what really matters—the only thing that matters.

Many people fear that if you preach grace you are going to end up minimizing sin and minimizing holiness. Yet the only hope for a holy, godly, and obedient life is to constantly be drenched in God's outpouring of grace. We only become holy as we acknowledge sin before the Father, and we can only acknowledge sin before the Father when we trust him to receive us without casting us out. Grace is what gives us the courage to bring our sin continually to the Father. Therefore, in one of the most beautiful paradoxes of the Bible, grace is our only hope for holiness. Likewise, grace is also our only power for holiness.

Our view of grace will only ever be as radical as our view of sin. Our sense of the need for grace will only ever be as great as our sense of the depth of our sin. It then follows that our love for Jesus will only ever be as rich as our awareness and appreciation of the work he has accomplished for us. Jesus said as much in Luke 7:36–50 when he told his disciples, "He who has been forgiven little loves little."

My Story of Grace

My entire life I have been a performer, whether it was academics or athletics or *watch me tie my shoe.* If I needed to bring my grades up in school I would just study harder. If I wanted to learn a new basketball skill I would just practice more. No matter what challenge I faced, my answer was just to try harder. Therefore, my lifelong assumption was that I could come through no matter what due solely to my application of the necessary level of self-effort. And I am ashamed to tell you that for a long time, it worked.

Until I became a Christian.

When my Christian life began, I bolted out of the blocks as if I had picked up another sport or hobby or subject. I dug in and tried hard. On many surface levels, it worked. I spent less time watching TV and more time reading God's Word. I had conversations with friends about Jesus and not just about basketball. I sought to pursue God through righteous living. But soon I noticed there were areas of sin in my life like fear and worry that were pretty stubborn and a lot harder to root out.

Nonetheless, I stuck to my tried and true methodology: I tried harder. Over time I began to realize the deep pride that results from so much self-effort. I fell into a pattern of minimizing my own sin and brokenness if it was not a sin I felt I could "deal with" in my own effort. It took God revealing areas of my life that no amount of effort could change—fear of failure, worry over finding a wife, anxiety over my future—to show me that the Christian life is not a self-reformation project where you expend copious effort merely to establish new habits.

By grace, over time I began to realize that the Christian life is a supernatural renovation from the inside out. It is about Christ in us giving us the confidence in our standing in him to face our brokenness and deep-rooted sin. It is about realizing our inability and declaring that he is the only one who will make us new. This was when the gospel began to be more precious to me. It was not only the good news that my foundation for acceptance before God was firm in Christ, but also the hope of true and lasting transformation of my heart and not merely my behaviors.

In my desperate need I began to see my Savior in a fresh light, and he became my everything. I began to understand the woman weeping at Jesus's feet, wetting them with her tears, drying them with her hair, kissing them with her lips, and anointing them with costly ointment (Luke 7:36–50). Trying harder for Jesus was replaced with actually *loving* Jesus.

The more we are aware of our sin's frequency and greatness and the more we experience God's grace in Christ despite our sin, the more the Spirit engenders a deep love in our hearts for Christ. It can never be a mere intellectual grasp of such love that changes us. Instead it is resting in the promise of Christ's finished work that actually activates the supernatural power that changes us. However, when we lose sight of the enormity of our sin, what follows is a diminishing appreciation for grace, which leaves very little love for the Savior (Luke 7:36–50). We know that those without Christ will never come to him unless they see their need. But what we often forget is that those of us who know Christ will never *keep coming* to Christ for transforming grace unless we are equally aware of our ongoing sin problem.

Chapter 2 Summary

- Grace theorized offers little comfort.
- Grace welcomes messes because grace is equipped to deal with them. Therefore grace-filled churches will be messy churches because they prove themselves to be a safe place for transformation.
- Our sense of our need for grace will only ever be as great as our sense of the depth of our sin.

Reflection Questions

1. To what degree do you find yourself struggling to find or maintain joy in the Christian life?
2. Do you ever think or act like an orphan? Like figuring life out is all up to you?
3. How does it feel to imagine God, the Ultimate Dance Partner, inviting you to a daily, ongoing dance with him? If possible, list three adjectives.
4. Interact with this erroneous statement: The message the non-Christian most needs to hear is grace; the message the Christian most needs to hear is discipleship.

3

WHAT IF GRACE IS NOT UNCONDITIONAL?

Likely we've all heard that grace is unconditional. What if I were to suggest that's not exactly true? Grace is beautifully unmerited and undeserved, but it is actually, in one sense, not unconditional. As Pastor Tim Keller masterfully summarized in his book *Counterfeit Gods*, "If you want God's grace, all you need is need, all you need is nothing. But that kind of spiritual humility is hard to muster."[5] We receive grace simply by humbling ourselves. We get grace simply by acknowledging there is absolutely nothing we can do to get it for ourselves. Author Gloria Furman put it well: "God is inviting you every day to wake up and say 'I can't do this.'"[6]

The Present Value of the Blood of Christ

Francis Schaeffer was the first author I ever read who identified the solution to our day-in, day-out need as

---

[5] Tim Keller, *Counterfeit Gods* (New York: Penguin, 2009), 56.

[6] Gloria Furman on The Kindled Podcast, ep. 13 "God Isn't Testing You; An Invitation to Radical Dependence," April 16, 2018.

believers in terms of the present value of the blood of Christ. In other words, there is a *converting* value to the blood of Christ that any Christian hopes in, or they would not actually be a Christian! But there is also a continuous post-conversion power or value to the blood of Christ. As Christ was trusted for conversion, so Christ must continue to be trusted with the moment-by-moment brokenness and sinfulness of the flesh that every Christian faces every single day (Col. 2:6–7). This *present value* of the blood of Christ is what saved Schaeffer from despair as a believer; it is what kept him in the faith. You see, he almost ditched the whole faith (just like me). In the Preface to *True Spirituality*, Schaeffer writes, "I searched through what the Bible said concerning reality as a Christian. Gradually I saw that the problem was that with all the teaching I had received after I was a Christian, I had heard little about what the Bible says about the meaning of the finished work of Christ for our present lives. Gradually the sun came out and the song came."[7]

As Christ was trusted for conversion, so Christ must continue to be trusted with the moment-by-moment brokenness and sinfulness of the flesh that every Christian faces every single day.

Schaeffer is saying that even as a pastor, no one had ever told him how to actually live the Christian life in light of the ongoing work of Christ. And then one day, by God's grace, Schaeffer understood the *present* value to the blood of Christ—could it be that this is what our hearts need to hear or hear afresh again?

[7] Francis Schaeffer, *True Spirituality* (Carol Stream, Illinois: Tyndale House, 2001), xxix–xxx.

If you are married, the act of becoming married did not happen until the actual moment you allowed the ring to be placed on your finger and said "I do." You were not married when you went on your first date or when you got serious or even when you got engaged. You were married at a singular point in time. But for that marriage to have life and growth, that commitment needs to be lived out on a daily basis in a thousand small (and sometimes large) ways.

It is the same way with Christ. We are not a Christian until we say "I do" to the converting power of the blood, but we must *keep saying* "I do" to Jesus with respect to his saving work as it applies to our day-in, day-out lives and circumstances. As Schaeffer emphasized, just as Mary cried out in Luke 1:38, our heart's continual cry must be, "Let it *be done* to me according to your word."[8] The Christ-follower is meant to thrive spiritually by continually receiving and resting in the promises of God's grace.

But in our marriage to our Bridegroom, Jesus, it is he who is the faultless, unfailing partner, continually wooing and romancing us so that our hearts do not just begrudgingly respond to his, but delight to respond and to honor him.

Who Will Deliver Me from This Body of Death?

The present value of Christ's blood isn't merely a New Testament concept; it has existed since the fall and is perhaps illustrated most clearly in an obscure and little-understood story from the book of Numbers. But first, a little background.

The book of Numbers begins with the people of God being, well, numbered. As they are about to enter

---

[8] HCSB

the Promised Land, the purpose of the census is both to count the fighting men and distribute allotments of land according to tribes. God's people, Israel, have been through a lot at this point. They have witnessed the ten plagues poured out upon Egypt and seen God act in tangible ways to save them from slavery and oppression. They were delivered through the Red Sea and saved from Pharaoh and his pursuing chariots. Then time and again, when the people felt desperate in the wilderness, God showed himself in mighty ways, providing food and water and direction.

In Numbers 13 and 14, right at the beginning of their time in the wilderness, God has Moses send spies to bring back a report of the Promised Land. All but two, Caleb and Joshua, are so overwhelmed with anxiety that they stir the people into a fearful frenzy. God then threatens to destroy the entire nation and start over. Moses repeats back to God his own promises to be slow to anger and abounding in steadfast love. So God again forgives the Old Testament church for her stubborn unbelief, for refusing to trust him and go with him, and even at times choosing to go with idols of her own making. But this time God does not forgive without consequence. In Numbers 14:21–23 God vows that no one from this unbelieving generation—with the exception of Caleb and Joshua—will enter the Promised Land. Israel will now wander for forty years in the wilderness until the unbelieving generation passes away.

Numbers 21 and Is There More to the Christian Life?

Finally we arrive at Numbers 21, a passage I find pivotal in answering the question asked in the hearts of many discouraged and disheartened Christians: *Is there more to the Christian life than what I'm experiencing?* To answer, we will compare two passages, Numbers 21: 4–9 and John 3:16, and examine their parallelism. My prayer is that this work will draw distinct parallels to our own individual experiences and grant us hope for the day in and day out of the Christian life.

After nearly forty years of wandering, the new generation of Israelites is on the verge of entering the Promised Land. Will the next generation believe and behave differently? Will the forty years in the wilderness have made a difference between the hearts of the children and the hearts of their parents and grandparents? In Numbers 21:4–9 we find the people are becoming impatient—again. They again express resentment toward Moses for God having taken them out of Egypt, and they grumble and complain about the provision—how they are growing tired of manna and tired of having to ask God for water. In verses 6–9, God does a curious thing:

> Then the LORD sent fiery serpents among the people, and they bit the people, so that many people of Israel died. And the people came to Moses and said,
>
> "We have sinned, for we have spoken against the LORD and against you. Pray to the LORD, that he take away the serpents from us." So Moses prayed for the people. And the LORD said to Moses, "Make a fiery serpent and set it on a pole, and everyone who is bitten, when he sees it, shall live." So Moses made a bronze serpent and set it on a pole. And if a serpent bit anyone, he would look at the bronze serpent and live.

It may seem strange to us that God would have them fashion a snake on a pole, yet that is precisely what God does. Author and Bible teacher Jen Wilkin offers the clearest exposition I have seen to date, tracing the symbol of the serpent on a pole through the meta-narrative of Scripture.[9] We—with New Testament eyes—know of the fullness and completion of all God's promises in the fact that God's Son, the perfect and sinless Jesus, hung in our stead on a pole, bringing to completion many Old Testament promises and upending death's curse. In Deuteronomy 21:22–23 we see for the first time that a hanged man is cursed by God. Later, Joshua calls for the hanging of the wicked king of Ai in Joshua 8, and in 2 Samuel 18 David's son, the rebellious and murderous Absalom, mistakenly hangs himself in an oak tree from the back of his mule as the mule walks on. In the New Testament we see that it is the very religious leaders themselves who have conformed to the symbol of evil: "You brood of vipers!" Jesus decries the religious leaders in Matthew 3:7, 12:34, 23:33, and Luke 3:7.

Yet it is Christ himself who goes to hang on the pole in our stead. We, who were born in sin, heirs of the serpent, are represented on that pole by Jesus, effectively receiving the transfer of our inheritance to his glorious kingdom of light (Acts 26:18). Wilkin notes it is utter foolishness to picture Christ as a serpent. But because he absorbed our utter depravity, we inherit his utter righteousness. "Christ redeemed us from the curse of the law by becoming a curse for us—for it is written, 'Cursed is everyone who hangs on a tree'" (Gal. 3:13). The serpent on the pole was a symbol of the One who was to be made sin for us (2 Cor. 5:21). On the cross Jesus became sin and was lifted up in our place so that the work of the serpent

---

[9] Jen Wilkin, "Saved By a Snake?" TGC Podcast, February 24, 2023.

of old might be overcome (Gen. 3:1–5, 15; 1 John 3:8; Rev. 20:2, 10). Whoever looks to Jesus in repentance and faith will be saved from the penalty of sin, from its power, and ultimately from its very presence.

Yes, this easily-overlooked account from Numbers 21 is more pivotal than we could imagine. But to fully understand its significance we have to move forward in redemptive history to an old faithful of stadium signs, sidewalk evangelists, and high school yearbook quotations: John 3:16. For many, it may conjure up sweet memories as comforting and familiar as the lines of "Amazing Grace" or the Doxology. But for the discouraged Christian, the anesthetic of John 3:16 may be so familiar that it does little to assuage present hurt and sorrow. For all eternity, sure—sign me up. But what about for the here and now?

Numbers 21 through the Eyes of John 3

A strong argument could be made that John 3:16 is the most well-known and often-quoted verse in the entire Bible. Yet most people seem to think it stands alone—adrift in a book that has little to do with its succinct gospel message packaging. But when we see that John 3:16 begins with the word "for," ("gar," in Greek, an explanatory conjunction and close kin to "since, then, or indeed") we know that John 3:16 is simply building on a previous point, which we find in John 3:14–15. What is going on here? John is adding flesh to the description. What is so important that it must be expanded upon?

In John 3, the respected teacher and leader Nicodemus, a member of the brood of vipers from Matthew 3:7, asks Jesus to explain being born again. He says, "How can these things be?" But Jesus turns

Nicodemus's question back to him, probing him to answer the question for himself: "Are you the teacher of Israel and yet do not understand these things?" I don't know about you, but I would love to hear the tone of our Savior's voice there. Did the sinless Christ mock Nicodemus or answer him with demeaning sarcasm? Certainly not. Rather, could it be that Jesus's words to Nicodemus implied *C'mon Nicodemus, say it. You know it. You know the Scriptures. You know about the new heart and the new life and the new birth (Ezek. 36:25–27). You know about the promised Messiah. You know who I am. You know I am the way to rebirth.*

In a word, "You know what this is all about, Nicodemus: grace." To see this even more clearly, we must examine the parallelism that exists between John 3:16 and John 3:14–15. So let's examine his points side by side to find the parallels. For ease of comparison, in the following paragraphs, John 3:14–15 will be in *italics*, and John 3:16 will be in **bold**:

> *14 And as Moses lifted up the serpent in the wilderness,*
>
> **16 For God so loved the world,**

As a teacher and expert in the law, Nicodemus would have understood that "And as Moses lifted up the serpent in the wilderness," was just another act of God's lovingkindness, or his *hesed* (the Old Testament word for grace). From day one of the exodus, the Israelites were nothing but knuckleheads. But Nicodemus would have known that in spite of it all, God continually showed his grace, love, mercy, and kindness to Israel in the wilderness. They were God's covenant people. He chose them for the sake of his name, and his grace was so sure that his commitment to them was unconditional. Lifting up the object of belief—the serpent in Numbers 21 or the Christ at the crucifixion—reveals the reality of God's grace and lovingkindness. In John 3:16 we find that grace extended to not just his people (as in ethnic Israel) but to all the knuckleheads of the world. For God so loved the world indeed.

The next set of verses read:

[14] so must the Son of Man be lifted up,

[16] that he gave his only Son,

Verse 14 begins with a "must," or what is known as a divine imperative, or another example of a grace-only solution to a "no-way-out situation." The only salvation for the Israelites in Numbers 21 was God's promise regarding the serpent being lifted up, that everyone who was bitten and looked at the serpent would live. In the same way, for all of mankind, the only way out after being bitten with the fatal venom of sin was the Son of Man being lifted up. But just as the people of Israel who were bitten had to believe the promise in order to experience the power of the promise, the only way the work of the cross is beneficial to us is if we believe (Heb. 4:1–3). If we continue in our unbelief, we will perish just as the people in Israel with the serpents would perish if they did not look in faith.

In the next set of phrases we see:

[15] that whoever believes in him

[16] that whoever believes in him

Evident in this precise parallelism in the ESV is the centrality of belief in Jesus. Evil will seek to get us to add to it, to tack on requirements or stipulations or qualifications, but it is simple belief in the Son of God that is our hope in this life and the next. Though belief is simple, in actuality it can feel anything but simple, as the belief Jesus requests is no mere intellectual assent. Rather it is a whole-hearted belief that involves our minds, our emotions, our deepest longings, and our wills. When Jesus is pursued by a crowd in John 6:28–29, they ask him, "What must we do, to be doing the works of God?" Jesus answers plainly, "This is the work of God, that you believe in him who he has sent." Jesus could have said anything as our primary work or responsibility, but he said the thing that cannot be ignored is *belief*. The daily work unto salvation is to believe. Both uses of the verb "believes" are in the present tense. We keep on continually believing in Christ—not just for conversion, but for transformation as well. Of course, even this "work" of believing is ultimately a gift of God's grace (Eph. 2:8–9), which we see in the parallel verses below.

Belief in Jesus is no mere intellectual assent. Rather it is a whole-hearted belief that involves our minds, our emotions, our deepest longings, and our wills.

[15] may have eternal life.

[16] should not perish but have eternal life.

Most Bible-believing followers of Christ naturally apply these verses to conversion, but they fail to apply them to the Holy Spirit and his work of progressively calling us into and enabling or empowering us for further sanctification. Eternal life does not begin when we die in Christ. Eternal life begins at conversion, making salvation both critical (occurring at a point in time) *and* progressive (happening continually or gradually). The New Testament speaks of us having been saved (critical, saved from the penalty of sin), being saved (progressively from the power of sin in sanctification), and yet-to-be saved (only when we are glorified at the resurrection being saved from the very presence of sin).

I See the Parallels . . . But What Do They Mean?

This Promise-Keeping God saved the Israelites from the serpents (their here-and-now), but in the specifics of the story, what he also did was point forward to the sure hope of what Christ would do for them on the cross.

It is the same with us.

What grace to be on this side of the cross and see the fulfillment of Christ's effectual death. But believer in Jesus, *take heart, there is so much more to come.* He is likewise pointing us forward.

This very day we are being prepared for a far greater reality—a hope that no eye has seen nor ear has heard, a hope that is as sure for us (and those Israelites!) as the cross was for the Israelites when they could only see their salvation from the serpents. God is continually pointing forward, upward, promising . . . and all the while revealing that he can be trusted to come through. John 3:16 authenticates what came before it—Numbers 21, which in turn authenticates our hope in eternity in heaven with Christ, which gives me great hope for today.

When my son, Josh, was twelve he was obsessed with the Gameboy game, SuperMarioKart. He played and played that game. He was just bent on winning it. For weeks we rode his emotional roller coaster at having almost beat it. He was continually frustrated, then excited, frustrated, then excited. One day as he and I were in the car, shoulder to shoulder, out of nowhere Josh erupted into crazed happiness. "I did it, dad! I finally won the game." I celebrated with him, high fives and smiles all around. A few moments later as we were coming down from the emotional high I thought it might be interesting to ask him, "How does it make you feel?" Of course he was happy and had a sense of having conquered the game. "Do you know why it feels so good?" I followed up, "It's because you just got a slight taste of what it's going to be like when we finally get to heaven. God wants us to experience total victory, total joy, and a complete sense of overcoming, and you just basically got a taste of entering the new Jerusalem." For my son, Josh, it was about far more than beating a Gameboy game; it was about God giving him (us!) a taste of true hope.

> It was the Unicorn who summed up what everyone was feeling . . . "I have come home at last! This is my real country! I belong here. This is the land I have been looking for all my life, though I never knew it til now. The reason why we loved the old Narnia is that it sometimes looked a little like this . . . Come further up! Come further in!" (C. S. Lewis, *The Chronicles of Narnia, The Last Battle*)

Chapter 3 Summary

- Grace is counterintuitive. We get it simply by acknowledging there is absolutely nothing we can do to get it for ourselves (James 4:6).
- The blood of Christ is sufficient both for our salvation (once for all time) and our sanctification (ongoing, day-by-day until we join Jesus in heaven).

Reflection Questions

1. Do you ever find yourself attempting to earn God's grace or "stay in" his grace?
2. How does it feel to interact with the statement, "We get grace simply by acknowledging there is absolutely nothing we can do to get it for ourselves."
3. After reading Numbers 21 in conjunction with John 3, how does 2 Corinthians 5:21 impact you? (God "made him [Jesus] sin who knew no sin, so that in him we might become the righteousness of God.")
4. Does reflecting on 2 Corinthians 5:21 motivate you toward any specific changes or choices reflective of lived-out godliness?

4

EVERY CHRISTIAN HAS A DANCE (WHAT'S YOURS?)

The message of hope that we explored in the previous chapter is not unique to just this book. No, this grace message is everywhere. So why do we have such a hard time hearing it?

As the capital-C Church, we can tend to overcomplicate the message of grace as it relates to our daily Christian lives. I hope to cut through this muddiness with the simplicity of a concept I've come to call the Gospel Waltz. It is a continuous, three-step dance with Christ, and through it we freshly experience the power of the gospel as an ongoing part of our daily lives.

When we examine the preaching of Jesus (Mark 1:15), the preaching of Peter (Acts 2:38), the inspired writings of Paul, the scholarship of Luther (95 Theses, Thesis #1), and many more throughout history, it becomes clear that all change begins with *repentance.* That is why the first step of the Waltz is *Repent.* In Numbers 21 we saw that the Israelites' hope began as God granted them repentance and they confessed, "We have sinned" (Num. 21:7). But just as God did not leave them in a rut of sin and repentance but provided the pathway to fresh faith, we too must likewise look with hope to the next step. Seeing our sin leads to a fresh need to gaze upon Christ in faith, which is the second step, *Believe*. In Numbers 21:8–9 we read that Israel was to "see" the bronze serpent and "look at" it. In the Believe step we exercise faith to both affirm our identity in Christ and to appropriate the transforming power of the blood of Christ to change our hearts and give us new desires and affections for his will and his ways.

Just as the Israelites' look of faith activated and released supernatural power to neutralize physical snake poison, the look of faith to Jesus activates the supernatural and transforming power of the blood of Christ. But it was far more than a mechanical "looking." It was the look of true faith, trust, and belief in the Lord's promise. The Hebrew words utilized in Numbers 21:8–9 shows us they intently regarded with favor and pleasure the surprising symbol of God's promise—in this case, the serpent on the pole. We must not miss the reality that the Israelites' only recourse from the literal poison coursing through their veins was repentance and acknowledgment of their need. Their only hope was to trust in the grace of God, which was connected to his promises and manifested as a bronze serpent on a pole. When a bitten Israelite looked in faith at the bronze serpent, a miracle occurred: poison was neutralized, power was released from heaven, and people were delivered from death. In the same way, as we live the Christian life moment by moment and as we become aware of sin, we not only repent, but also believe the gospel afresh. We trust power from heaven to be released in our lives at the very place of our repentance based on the promises of God.

Finally, any waltz sequence is incomplete without the third step. So, having believed the gospel of grace afresh, we are now equipped with new power to step into the fight against sin and the fight for righteousness—hence the third step of the Gospel Waltz is to *Fight*. We're told in Numbers 21:8–9 that any Israelite who was bitten and looked in faith "lived." There is indeed a life to live for the follower of Christ. The fruit of faith in the transforming grace of God is a new desire to say no to sin and yes to righteousness (Titus 2:11–12). We are called to *Repent*, *Believe*, and *Fight*. The Gospel Waltz offers a simple paradigm to confused believers who are left wondering what the Spirit-filled life really is. If any step is left out of the dance, it is no longer a waltz. The Repent Step keeps us from falling into self-righteousness. The Believe Step keeps us from falling to self-effort or self-reliance. The Fight Step keeps us from falling into self-indulgence. It is all three steps, all the time, or it is not a waltz. It is a continuous, three-step dance with Jesus that leads to a fresh outpouring of the transforming power of grace.

> *The Waltz is a continuous, three-step dance with Jesus that leads to a fresh outpouring of the transforming power of grace.*

If we can approach learning the steps of the Gospel Waltz as a tool by which we engage Christ through the gospel on a daily basis, we will see that none of us approaches the three steps of the Waltz in an even-footed way. We are all by nature heavy-footed in one of the steps. Some of us are heavy-footed repenters. Others are heavy-footed in the Believe step (though, in my experience, this is very rare). Finally, still others are heavy-footed in the Fight step. Heavy-footedness results from temperament, family background, emotional or psychological brokenness, books you've read, wounds you've experienced—the list goes on. And it all adds up to a tendency to place undue emphasis on one of the three steps of the Gospel Waltz: Repent, Believe, or Fight.

Like any athlete, musician, or preacher who reviews their video or audio after a game, concert, or sermon in order to identify weaknesses and improve for the future, recognizing our heavy-footedness reveals imbalances that might trip us up as we seek to abide in Christ. The difference, however, is we are not identifying weaknesses so we can "do better at the next performance." Our dance with Jesus is not a dance of performance, but a dance of delight. Our dance partner is the one who both begins and sustains the dance, so our "skills" at the Gospel Waltz are entirely a gift rather than a muscle we've flexed or a step we've fixed.

Whether we realize it or not, all Christians dance. Let's examine a few of the dances we tend to employ in our own efforts to try to make life work.

The Bunny Hop

Some people approach the Christian life as a one-step dance: the Bunny Hop. You may have heard of this classic line dance created by The Ray Anthony Orchestra in the early 1950s. Often present at large events, the familiar two taps right, two taps left, jump forward, jump back, and "hop, hop, hop" may seem like a thing of the past, but it is not as out of vogue as we might think. Bunny Hoppers reduce the Christian life to one single element, which is very often: *try harder*. Instead of hop, hop, hop, it's *recommit, recommit, recommit*. I have even heard it preached as "Fight!

Fight! Fight! With all your might!" almost to the cadence of a marching soldier. In this type of dancing a believer acknowledges that Christ got them started, but they think that now it is up to them to maintain or improve their standing with God, and the only option is to try harder.

The Nike slogan "Just Do It" may sell shoes, but in the Christian life "Just Do It" just doesn't cut it. It puts the cart of effort before the horse of our identity in Christ, mandating the imperative before the indicative, commanding peak performance from a fuel-less car. Throughout all of Scripture, but notably in Paul's epistles, we see the opposite pattern: the indicative (what is true about God, the gospel, and of us as his children) before the imperative (this is how we should live in light of what is true about God and us in Christ).

Another variation of the Bunny Hop is *Confess. Confess. Confess.* These folks tend to think that finding what they are looking for in the Christian life is about rooting out more sin. If only they repented more deeply, they think, then they would find joy. Still another variation is "let go, let God." These Bunny Hoppers think that their problem with lack of joy in the Christian life has to do with a failure to be completely yielded and surrendered to the process. If they would just stop trying so hard and begin resting more, they would find what they are looking for.

Still another version of the Bunny Hop or One-Step is seen in those who think the key to the "victorious" Christian life is found in constantly reciting our identity in Christ. In extreme forms, such individuals have a hard time even admitting they are sinners because they believe the key to change is constantly affirming that they are not sinners but saints. They focus so much on their positional righteousness in Christ that they fail to truly see their daily condition of sinfulness before God's holiness and their constant need for a Savior.

Clearly the Bible calls us to confess our sins, rest in Christ's finished work, affirm our identity in Christ, and strive after holiness, but the Christian life is not reducible to one individual step.

The Texas Two-Step

Beyond the Bunny Hop, other folks prefer the Texas Two-Step. There are three variations of the Texas two-step: 1) the more popular Confess and Try Harder, 2) the well-known Trust and Obey and 3) the less prevalent (but slightly more biblical) Repent and Believe. All three versions appear more balanced than the Bunny Hop, but both leave us incomplete and hobbling in our walk with Jesus.

Confess and Try Harder

The Confess and Try Harder Two-Step is simply a more layered *try harder* Bunny Hop. It is the Repent and Fight steps of the Waltz without the Believe step, and while it incorporates an element of repentance, there is far more to the Christian life than acknowledging our sin and gutting it out. This particular two-step sounds something like: "I am a Christian. I am called to obey God's commands. Therefore, I'm going to obey God's commands." And then you fail. So you say, "Well, I've got to obey God's commands. I'll ask his forgiveness, promise not to do what I did or didn't do ever again, and then I'm going to try harder." But then you fail again. Then one of two things happens: you either fall into despair because no matter how hard you try, life just isn't changing the way you expected it would, or on the other extreme, you slip into self-righteousness because you think, "Hey, I'm actually doing this. I'm actually living the life. Why can't others just step it up?"

Confess and Try Harder skips the crucial element of believing in Christ for transforming power; it de-supernaturalizes the Christian life. If you think about it, there is actually no Jesus in this Texas Two-step. Anyone can experience regret over their failures and then recommit to do better. What makes the Christian life distinctively Christian is our continual hope in Christ, not in self.

Trust and Obey (Believe and Fight)

Another variation of the two-step involves affirming our identity in Christ and then seeking to live out that identity by trying hard to live up to it. Clearly we are called to affirm our identity in Christ, but we also must appropriate the present power of the blood of Christ to change us at the point of our repentance. Often, however, this two-step leaves out the need to repent as well as the need to appropriate the power of the gospel to change us. This dance flows from a tendency to focus so much on identity in Christ that acknowledging the presence of indwelling sin is often absent. The "flesh" as Paul calls it, is irreformable and will never decrease in this life (Rom. 7:14–25; Gal. 5:16). Theologian A.A. Hodge sums it up when he says, "innate moral corruption remains in the regenerate as long as they live."[10] However, as we repent of our sin and appropriate the present value of the blood

---

[10] A.A. Hodge, *The Westminster Confession: A Commentary* (Edinburgh: Banner of Truth, 1988), 115.

of Christ, our capacity to say no to the flesh increases. Finally, the Trust and Obey (Believe and Fight) two-step is still prone to leave us in the paradigm of self-effort as we affirm our identity and just try harder. Two-stepping in this manner makes it convenient to avoid hard conversations, the pain of God searching our hearts (Ps. 139:23–24), and the need for true humility and change.

Confess and Believe

The third variation of the Texas two-step is Confess and Believe, or only the Repent and Believe steps of the Gospel Waltz, omitting the Fight step. Of all the false dances we employ to make life work, this is the most closely biblical, fooling us into thinking that we are actually waltzing. Confess and Believe takes seriously our need to acknowledge sin in humility and admit our need for grace, and it hopes, trusts, and continually believes in Christ. There is, however, one downside to the Confess and Believe dance that prevents it from being holistically biblical: it often downplays the biblical imperatives of obedience and discipleship.

This truncated dance is why some who hear about "grace-driven churches" are tempted to cringe. It seems at times that when people have a "grace awakening" they can begin to minimize obedience, discipleship, holiness, and godliness. They focus on grace only as unconditional love and fail to see grace *also* as supernatural, transforming power. We see this "both/and" integration in Paul's epistles where the first part of what Paul writes to a given church emphasizes the wonderful truths of the gospel of grace, and then the latter part of the letter emphasizes the highly ethical fruit of the gospel of grace. If we fail to emphasize the gospel call that there is indeed a life to live and God's holiness to pursue, and if we fail to teach the gospel empowerment and enabling for such a life, we fail to teach the whole gospel.

These two elements of grace—unconditional love and transforming power—keep us from becoming unbalanced in our Christian walk. We cannot have one without the other. Without them, either variation of the Texas Two-Step will inevitably lead to failure: either through self-despair or self-righteousness. God longs to save us from these pitfalls. Before we dive into the three steps of the Waltz, however, it is important to acknowledge the final and most deceptive dance that Christians engage in, often without even realizing they are doing so: the Orphan Waltz.

The Orphan Waltz

My good friend Tim Bennett of Gospel Tree Ministries and I have taught the Gospel Waltz together for years, and he has coined an especially helpful phrase which he calls the Orphan Waltz. The three steps of the Orphan Waltz would be "Defend! Disbelieve! Do!" The Orphan Waltz follows the pattern of Adam and Eve in Genesis 3. When his sin is exposed, Adam defends himself and blames the woman instead of repenting, and the woman defends herself and blames the serpent instead of repenting. When we go through life with an orphan mentality, we fail to see ourselves as God's beloved children, secure in Christ. As a result, we feel the need to build and *defend* our own record of righteousness instead of resting in Christ's righteousness. This leads to a lifestyle of defending ourselves through blame shifting, excuse making and playing the victim. Then, rather than believing the gospel in a time of failure and brokenness, the orphan response is to *disbelieve* the Gospel and believe in lies, because an orphan believes there is no one out there to care for them beyond themselves. The Orphan Mentality holds to the dictum: If it's to be, it's up to me. Finally, since the orphan does not have hope in any power but self, the only choice left for him is to *do* better, and we are back to Nike Christianity all over again.

The aim of the Orphan Waltz is not gospel transformation through responding as sons and daughters to the music of God's loving pursuit of our hearts through the circumstances, situations, and relationships of life. Instead, the aim of the Orphan Waltz is to try to stop the music altogether. An individual struggling with orphan mentality just wants things to get better rather than embracing the opportunity for transformation by the power of grace.

Earlier we considered the fundamentals of a grace-driven life. We need to realize that the Orphan Mentality follows its own set of fundamentals:

- I am in control of my own destiny.
- I am on my own.
- I must work hard for acceptance.
- No one has my best interest at heart.
- I am the only person I can trust.
- I can't let anyone see my weaknesses.

We must understand that when the pressure is on, we tend to operate not out of our carefully-constructed theological presuppositions, but out of the functional belief system of our brokenness. When we face stress, we tend to turn toward what we most want in life: the idols that we believe will give us the security, significance, comfort, and peace we deeply desire. Rather than believing our deepest desires will be met through intimacy with our Heavenly Father who deeply loves us, we look elsewhere for what only God can give us. We look for God-substitutes to give us what only intimacy with God can offer. Another word for this is idolatry. In *Counterfeit Gods*, Tim Keller describes an idol as "anything more important to you than God, anything that absorbs your heart and imagination more than God, and anything that you seek to give you what only God can give."[11] To help us get in touch with the idols of our own hearts, the following questions are often helpful:

- What pushes your "hot button"?
- What stresses you out?
- What brings you the most happiness/sadness?
- What are your worst-case scenarios in life?
- What monopolizes your prayers?

While the Orphan Waltz is technically a waltz made up of three steps, for Christians it is the most vicious type of false dance because it twists and churns each step of the Gospel Waltz into unrecognizable self-reliance and unbelief. It is the most menacing of the false dances because while it feels legitimate with three steps, it taunts God at every turn: false repentance, pseudo-belief, and self-sufficient fighting.

Of course, we know that an orphan is one who lacks a father and mother, or even anyone to truly care for them, and who is forced to figure out life all

---

[11] Timothy Keller, *Counterfeit Gods: The Empty Promises of Money, Sex, and Power, and the Only Hope That Matters* (New York: Riverhead Books, 2011), xix.

on their own. Within our paradigm, the Orphan Waltz is danced by one who is acting as if there is no Savior, no Father God who loves them, no family they are a part of, and therefore no one they can count on besides themselves. Because the Orphan Waltzer thinks there is no dance partner, the waltzer is left to do things for him or herself. Perhaps this sounds familiar . . . or even comfortable? Our great hope when we find ourselves living as orphans and engaging in the three steps of the Orphan Waltz is knowing that the Father's heart is drawn to orphans. "Religion that is pure and undefiled before God the Father is this: to visit orphans and widows in their affliction" (James 1:27). If God delights in the practice of faith that visits orphans, then clearly his own heart is drawn not just to literal orphans, but also to those of us who think and even act like orphans. The very Jesus who promised us in John 14:18, "I will not leave you as orphans," is the same Jesus who indeed gets us. And because of this all-encompassing and radical pursuit we have "received the Spirit of adoption as sons, by whom we cry, 'Abba! Father!'" (Rom. 8:15).

Come and See the Beauty

All true believers agree that Christ must be preached as the only hope for the non-Christian. But what we sometimes fail to focus on as much is that Christ must also be preached as the only hope for the *Christian*. If Jesus is not presented as the only moment-by-moment way forward for believers, we will fall into a powerless dance of self-reliance and often end up turning our backs on Christ and looking to other things for relief. No matter which way we turn, when our path is away from Christ we are promised to find saltwater or a mouthful of dry gravel that will leave us thirstier still. But how do we become a people who lift Christ up for all (including ourselves) to see? And moreover, how do we do so from a place of gratitude and not obligation, from a secure foundation not based on our own effort?

We waltz.

Now a caution: *waltzing is not going to fix us.* If you are looking for the "victorious Christian life," or a higher life movement, you have come to the wrong place. There is no such thing. But that is actually hopeful! For there is nothing, not a single thing, outside of Christ's transforming power in our lives that holds any promise of lasting change. I don't know about you, but that helps my heart to stop looking for anything more apart from Christ. Since waltzing can never fix us, it actually opens opportunity for us to see how it can *serve* us. Waltzing is simply how broken people with broken lives live in a broken world, yet experience substantial healing, until Christ returns.

If Jesus is not presented as the only moment-by-moment way forward for believers, we will fall into a powerless dance of self-reliance and often end up turning our backs on Christ and looking to other things for relief.

But, But, But . . .

As we consider the various incomplete dances Christians engage in, we must acknowledge the beauty of the desire behind them. All Christians know that we are called to Christ-likeness. Believers understand it is our destiny to become godly and to live obedient lives. No Christ-follower who understands their Bible debates whether believers are called to holiness. However, what *is* hotly debated is the on-ramp to holiness—how we get there.

As I emphasize grace as both the motivation and empowerment for godliness, I am often surprised that some respond initially with just one word: *but.* But . . . what about effort? But . . . what about striving after obedience? But . . . what about a rigorous application of the will to the commandments of God? But . . . But . . . But . . . I want to respond with another, most significant "but":

> But what about the supernatural nature of the gospel? Do we truly believe it?

We are speaking of the gospel of grace as both the message of God's unconditional love and the message of God's supernatural, transforming power. Because the truth is no Christian will ever be truly holy as Christ is holy unless it is a holiness enabled by grace and by the power of the Holy Spirit.

In April 2017, *The New York Times* reported on the death of an extraordinary man, Eugene Lang. A prominent businessman, investor, and self-made millionaire, Mr. Lang made a spur-of-the-moment decision in 1981 while giving the commencement address to a group of sixth graders at a school in East Harlem. During the address to the largely-underprivileged students, Mr. Lang found himself questioning why these students were ever going to listen to him. "It dawned on me that the commencement banalities I planned were completely irrelevant."

Mid-speech, Mr. Lang scrapped his talk and spoke from the heart. He promised college scholarship money to each student admitted to a four-year college. The initial shock and overwhelm at Mr. Lang's generous gesture was quickly met with the realities of the students' difficult circumstances. Even the school principal told Mr. Lang he thought it would be great if one or two students made it to take him up on the scholarships. But after Mr. Lang's offer, the class was never the same. Over half of those students graduated from high school, and nearly half of the class took him up on his offer. The students said their success was because they had hope; they had something to look forward to. They had been promised the resources, and that motivated them to work out of love and hope for that promise to be fulfilled.

The story is a metaphor, a shadow of the Christian life. What we possess in Christ is, yes, the idea of a future hope in heaven. But that stops short of the abundance we have been given, meaning the guarantee of supernatural empowerment via the Holy Spirit to motivate us in a path of righteousness and hope today.

Jesus Christ is our millionaire, and he has promised all the resources we need to live a holy life. He has handed over the keys to the kingdom—his promises—and given us all the hope we could ever want to fight against sin and to pursue godliness. It is not mere natural motivation that helps us want to know God's goodness and provision. Grace is not just a philosophical concept that if we "get it" motivates us to live better. Grace "works" because grace is a supernatural power, not a human concept! Grace by definition will change lives but it also must be appropriated. Mr. Lang's financial promise gave hope and resources, without which it would have been nearly impossible for those students to go to college. But the students also had to apply themselves. They had to put in the work to get the grades. When it comes to the unique relationship between grace and good works, it is a bit of a mystery for sure.

Don't Trip on the Mechanics

A waltz may have a 1-2-3- to it, but it is not a checklist. *Waltzing is relational, not mechanical.* We learn to waltz in order to experience a joyful dance with a partner—The Perfect Partner. We all know the difference between the mandatory fifth grade square dancing class where the partners are hesitant to touch in contrast to a groom gazing at his radiant bride on their wedding day, pulling her close for their first dance. The first is obligatory . . . stilted . . . awkward, and the second is joyful and dazzling. Waltzing is not a new key to unlock the secret of a changed life—though waltzing will result in a changed life. Waltzing is how we abide in Christ, how we experience the presence and power of the Holy Spirit on a continual basis, and how we are invited to share in his intimate joy.

I Hear Music

The idea of the Gospel Waltz likely falls differently on each of us. If at this point you feel yourself scratching your head, wondering what all the flap is about grace, please stick around. Others of us may be really gripped for the first time by the wonder and joy of being delighted in by a Father who treats us not according to our performance, our obedience, or even our faith, but who treats us as he would treat Christ himself (John 17:23), because we have been given his grace, the righteousness of Jesus (2 Cor. 5:21). Those in the grip of grace are beginning to understand and rest in the love the Father has for us (1 John 4:16), and it often feels like coming alive for the first time. Many have told me it feels like being converted all over again.

But others have received the gift of grace and are reaching into the box and realizing "Oh, there's another part of the present!" The other part is that grace is not merely a cup of warm milk. Grace is radically life-transforming. In other words, there is more to grace than simply being overjoyed that the Father delights in us; that delight supernaturally propels us into personal obedience and outward ministry. Many of us have too quickly forgotten that the Christian life is a supernatural life.

Finally, by God's grace, some are really gripped by and confident in the love of God, and so can say, "Yes, it's all true. God loves me, he delights in me, and his power toward me is fresh every day, so I can think about myself less and think upward and outward more." Ultimately, the goal of grace is a life of freedom to the glory of God. True humanity is not the freedom to do whatever you want. It is the freedom to delight in doing what God wants.

This is no fifth-grade dance. The Waltz we want to grow with and into is a smooth, integrated three-step dance with Christ through which we experience the joyful gaze of the groom embracing us, his beloved bride, no matter the circumstances of the ballroom we may find ourselves in. The distinct thing about any waltz is that it is not a one-step, or even a two-step, but a *three*-step. Let's examine together each of the steps that make up this continually flowing and balanced dance that describes the very essence of the Christian life.

Chapter 4 Summary

- We employ false dances to try to make life work by our own efforts.
- Christ is not merely the only hope for the non-Christian. Christ and his grace continues to be the only hope for the Christian as well.
- Waltzing can never fix us—waltzing is simply how broken people with broken lives live in a broken world yet experience substantial healing until Christ returns.
- Waltzing is how we abide in Christ, how we experience the presence and power of the Holy Spirit on a continual basis, and how we are invited to share in his intimate joy.

Reflection Questions

1. Though you may not thoroughly understand each of the steps of the Waltz yet, which step do you suspect you are heavy-footed in and how does that play out in your life?
2. Is there a two-step you practice?
3. What stirs in you as you reflect on the statement that waltzing won't fix you, but that it will lead to gradual transformation?
4. How and where have you been dancing the Orphan Waltz, struggling to believe that God's heart toward you is good?

5

REPENT: ALL CHANGE STARTS HERE

A father gifted a toy boat to his son with the condition that the boy could only play with the boat when his father was with him. Unable to contain himself, the boy took the boat to the lake without his father and played and played with the boat, stuffing it with leaves and small pebbles, careening it through the lapping waves. When the boy turned from gathering some small twigs to add as cargo, he realized it was gone, blown into deep water by the wind. The father heard his son's cries and came running. Quickly, the father snatched up some palm-sized stones lying on the side of the shore and began to hurl them into the air, directly toward the boat.

Though he was covered with shame and guilt, having ignored his father's instruction, the boy cried out, "Stop!" as huge tears welled in his eyes. The boy thought that his father, in anger and justice, was trying to destroy the boat as a consequence for his disobedience. "Stop, Daddy!" the boy cried. "You're going to destroy my boat!"

The father bent down and lovingly put his hands on his son's shoulders, causing the frantic boy to look back into his eyes.

"No, son, I'm not throwing rocks at your boat; I'm throwing them *beyond* your boat, trying to create stronger ripples that will push it back toward us."

Sadly, many of us see the call to repentance as a call to endure having rocks thrown at us instead of an invitation to restored joy and renewed life. As a result of all the misconceptions and misunderstandings we carry surrounding repentance, we must clarify the basics and redefine repentance as an invitation back into a restored relationship. But let's be clear from the start: the Father has not turned away from us, nor will he ever turn away from anyone in Christ. Rather, when we sin we have turned away from him. God turned away from Christ on the cross so that we might never fear him turning away from us. Our repentance flows from God having allowed us to see the depth of our need by allowing us to see just how much we can mess up in our own efforts. It is God's open arms, his gentle hand tilting our face back toward his; it is his way of inviting us back into fellowship with him. His kindness leads us to repentance (Rom. 2:4).

When my sense of guilt and shame disrupts my feeling of intimacy with the Father, I must recognize that he is the Father who is always looking to welcome the prodigal home (Luke 15:11–32). My sin causes me to put distance between God and me. God can handle our sin. He did, in Christ. But he chooses to wait on high for us to turn to him in repentance (Isa. 30:15–18)—not with promises to do better, not with a commitment to try harder, not with oaths not to mess up next time—but simply to say, "I have sinned" (Num. 21:7). Period. "Apart from your grace I'm most likely to do it again." Period. "I need mercy." Period. Repentance is collapsing into Christ out of utter need. And that is the first step of the waltz.

How Are We Exposed?

Repentance conjures up misery for many of us, doesn't it? It can bubble up intense feelings of sadness, guilt, and shame from memories of previous circumstances. Because of those previous experiences, or perhaps even because of wounding from instances where our true repentance was not well-received by others, it can be difficult for us not to see sadness, misery, guilt, and shame as the primary elements of repentance. But godly repentance has none of those as its end aim, for repentance is the actual true pathway to joy.

Furthermore, repentance conjures up misery because many of us tend to think that repenting is what "bad Christians" do. Many believers have adopted a paradigm of the Christian life that says the longer we walk with Jesus, the less we will be repenting. It is the very same tragic paradigm that says mature Christians sin less. It is also the perspective that is quick to believe God turns his back, walks away, crosses his arms in frustration, and wags his head in disgust when we sin. If we live within that paradigm, then to admit sin—to admit the need to repent—is giving in to the mindset that God is disgusted with us. Quite simply, that is just too painful for many to face, so repentance continues to conjure up misery.

I love God's Word, but I don't know about you, sometimes it is easier to admire it from afar. I remember once reading Psalm 119 and coming across verse 97: "Oh how I love your law!" When I read this, I was at a place in my Christian life where I was living in a particularly unhealthy performance paradigm, and I could absolutely not say that. How could I say I *loved* God's law? In my paradigm, all the law did was point out my failures and emphasize the distance between my Father and me. From this performance-driven outlook, all the law did was condemn me. Oh, not for eternity . . . I knew I was saved by Christ. But the law continued to condemn me in my moment-by-moment experience of intimacy with God. God's Word became overwhelming to me. How could I love something that made me feel like a miserable Christ-follower? It seemed that all the call to repentance did to me was make me feel condemned and filled with shame.

Not only does God's Word expose our sin, but countless situations, circumstances, and relationships also expose our sin. Even good things in our lives can expose sin. As we abide in Christ, we seek to moderate amounts of good things that are good for us in their place—beauty, work, relational intimacy, etc. But these same items quickly turn sinful when out of place or in excess. God uses both the good and the hard—including circumstances, relationships, and certainly the Scriptures—to expose us and invite us back to himself.

By 2022, like many pastors I had experienced tension at every turn throughout the Covid-19 pandemic. During the lockdown and beyond it felt as if none of us in leadership could make a decision that wouldn't anger half of our congregation. The elders knew I needed time off, and they were gracious to grant me a month of sabbatical to read Scripture, rest, and reflect with the Lord.

During my time away, the Lord patiently brought me to a place of conviction in regard to a nasty habit

I had developed. I realized that I had begun responding to tension as if I was a thermometer rather than a thermostat. Instead of actively working to lower the temperature in a given situation, I was allowing my people-pleasing sin bent to take command, and I became caught up in the heated emotion of the moment. As those around me communicated their views or disagreements with more intensity, God revealed to me that internally I was either boiling with anger, shot through with anxiety, or tempted to simply shut down and turn off.

How did I respond to God's prick of my heart? I waltzed. With the Lord's help I worked through the three steps of the Gospel Waltz: Repent, Believe, and Fight. I repented of my approval-addiction flesh. I believed the gospel truths that my identity is in Christ and not in what other people think about me. I also chose to appropriate the present, transforming, supernatural power of the blood of Christ to enable me to overcome my approval-addiction flesh, and I chose to engage in the fight against sin by choosing to believe my Father is pursuing my heart through all of this for his glory and my good. I waltzed in a fresh way and began to experience supernatural change.

But it's not just evil's pursuit of us through challenging circumstances that God wants to alert us to. We must also be alert to the wickedness within our own hearts. God sent the serpents upon the people in Numbers 21 so they would make the connection that the poison of asps or vipers was *within their own hearts*; it was killing them and they didn't even know it. The venom without was to draw attention to the venom within. In the same way vile venom spews from our mouths it can also spill from our hearts, poisoning us and all those within our influence. Bible teacher Paige Brown says that sin in the Bible is highly relational. Think adultery, prostitution, treachery, favoritism, or abandonment—all are ultimately heart issues. With this level of relational intensity, it follows that sin has a damaging reach. It hurts the people we love the most. But more than disgusting, sin is downright dangerous to us and to those we love, and the more we believe that, the more quickly and deeply we will repent.

But the good news is that God pursues us more intently than sin or evil ever does. He pursues us through circumstances, relationships, events, troubles, trials, and even through blessings. God is not being mean or throwing rocks at us as he moves our hearts toward him in repentance. No, it is just the opposite. As we see in Romans 2:4 it is God's kindness that leads us to repentance.

Yet, all of these kindnesses end up being pressure points, and they make us highly uncomfortable. Even if it is prosperity we are dealing with, the pressure point might become consequences of lethargy and the results of staying in our comfort zone, which will eventually become a boil. When the pressures of life explode, we become aware of the pus—the pride, unbelief, and self (self-reliance, self-indulgence, self-sufficiency, self-righteousness, and self-centeredness)—that was inside. We see our need to be cleaned up. We see our need for repentance.

God pursues us more intently than sin or evil ever does.

But whatever it is that exposes us, when we as Christians see our sin and are moved by the Holy Spirit, we have a choice to make. We must choose whether or not we will run to the Father, whose arms are always open wide, ready to help us deal with the intruder. We have the invitation to acknowledge our need by admitting our hopelessness to transform ourselves, and we can ask God to clean us up.

Godly Grief Versus Ungodly Grief

Scripture refers to different kinds of human grief as a response to sin. We see Judas express it after his betrayal of Jesus, and we also see it after Peter denies Jesus three times. Before we begin to examine godly repentance, it is again important to define what it is not. The good grief displayed in godly repentance needs parameters and boundaries so that it does not run amok and turn to ungodly grief. Good grief is true repentance as it leads us to experience supernatural transforming grace. Let's take a look at some attributes of ungodly grief and repentance:

Self-reformation. First off, repentance is not confessing your sin, telling God you are sorry, promising never to do it again, and then trying really hard to muster the effort and discipline necessary to pull off your commitment. There is way too much self, pride, and self-reliance for this path to even begin to resemble godly grief and repentance. It is actually quite arrogant to think we could do better next time through simply exerting greater effort!

Biblical repentance exhibits surrender and brokenness and contrition—a path where there is no confidence in self-reformation. True repentance says, "God, I'm sorry. And I make no promises to do better because unless you supernaturally transform me by your grace, I will end up giving into the same temptation again." True repentance acknowledges that we sin because we are sinners, not that we are sinners because we sin. In other words, the fruit sins of behaviors are not our biggest problem. The root sins of the heart are the deeper issue. True repentance acknowledges transformation occurs from the inside out and begins with the heart, not merely the will.

Lessening Frequency. It is completely unbiblical to think that the longer you have walked with Christ the less you will be repenting. In fact, the closer you grow to the light and the more familiar you become with the truths of Scripture, the more you will see the filthiness of your own garments.

I grew up in central Pennsylvania where my grandfather had a coal furnace. Regularly I would love to go down into the unfinished basement and help my grandfather shovel coal. When you are down in this type of basement there is no real light, and you can barely see your hand in front of your face. While you are in the basement you have no grasp of what you actually look like, but then you come up into the light and realize you are covered in soot.

That is the way the Christian life is apart from knowledge of the Word. You think you are ok. But the more we know of Scripture and the more years we spend walking with God, the more we see of our sin and the more we understand of God's holiness. Again it is the paradox of the garden—instead of becoming "like God," part of true Christian maturity is growth in the realization of how very unlike God we are.

Self-Loathing. Repentance is never self-hatred. Repentance never leads to despair. Repentance is mourning over your sin . . . deeply but *briefly*. Robert Murray M'Cheyne once said, "For every look at yourself, take ten looks at Christ."[12] The thought has evolved to mean for every glance at your sin, gaze ten times as long upon Christ. As we grieve enough to see our fresh need for Christ and gaze upon him and have our joy restored, Paul says then we have experienced godly grief (2 Cor. 7:8–11). One of the chief hindrances to deep repentance is actually shame and guilt. Repentance is not at all self-hatred—no, that would dishonor God the Creator. It does not lead to despair because God opposes the proud, but gives grace to the humble. If we truly choose to gaze ten times as long upon Christ for every single look upon our sin, repentance will always be a door to joy.

Flippancy. Conversely, if we are ever flippant about repentance, then we are not truly repentant either. True repentance longs for change, and a flippant heart reveals a low view of how bad our sin really is and a lack of belief in God's ability to make us new. True repentance bubbles up in the soul a deep desire for reformation of life, where all the power is attributable to God. God does the work, but if our hearts are not changed and if there is not a new desire and zeal for obedience and holy living, then we have not yet apprehended Christ the way we need to. We have not yet trusted in the power of the cross nor repented deeply of our sin. If we are repenting by the power of the Holy Spirit, our greatest grief is not over the consequences of our sin that we experience but instead over the realization that we have failed to love the God who loves us and redeemed us. How can we be flippant over sin when

---

[12] *Memoir and Remains of the Rev. Robert Murray McCheyne* (Edinburgh, 1984), 293.

we realize it is against our Father in Heaven? Grace is not cheap. It cost Jesus everything. Our sin put Jesus on the cross. How can we be flippant about something like that?

The Grace of Godly Grief

Now that we have established some of the threats to true repentance, what are the attributes of the kind of repentance that not only acknowledges our sin and brokenness but also leads us to experience supernatural transforming grace?

To find our answer we turn to Paul's second letter to the Corinthians. Second Corinthians is actually *Third* Corinthians as there is a Second Corinthians we don't have. Paul speaks in 2 Corinthians 7 about a previous letter he sent after what we know as First Corinthians, a painful letter in which he had to rebuke the church at Corinth for some gross sin or some kind of immorality in the church. He wrote what is now called 2 Corinthians as a follow-up to this painful letter.

Let's take a look at 2 Corinthians 7:8–13.

> For even if I made you grieve with my letter, I do not regret it—though I did regret it, for I see that that letter grieved you, though only for a while. As it is, I rejoice, not because you were grieved, but because you were grieved into repenting. For you felt a godly grief, so that you suffered no loss through us.
>
> For godly grief produces a repentance that leads to salvation without regret, whereas worldly grief produces death. For see what earnestness this godly grief has produced in you, but also what

> eagerness to clear yourselves, what indignation, what fear, what longing, what zeal, what punishment! At every point you have proved yourselves innocent in the matter. So although I wrote to you, it was not for the sake of the one who did the wrong, nor for the sake of the one who suffered the wrong, but in order that your earnestness for us might be revealed to you in the sight of God. Therefore we are comforted.

Paul says godly grief produces a repentance that leads to salvation. This is useful! This is even helpful! When was the last time we associated the words *useful* or *helpful* with grief? But it is true: being fully in touch with all that my sin does to me and to other people—seeing all that my sin costs me, and especially what it does to God's own heart—gives me energy to turn to God in true repentance. It is important to realize that Paul uses the word "salvation" in different ways in different contexts. It might be tempting to think that Paul is saying that repentance leads to deliverance from hell and the gift of conversion. But Paul is here talking to Christians who have already been converted. He is talking about us as believers entering into a fuller experience of our salvation in Christ through continued repentance. Paul also uses the present tense to communicate the truth that godly grief continually and constantly produces a repentance that leads to a deeper experience of salvation. Repentance is a way of life for the Christian that leads us ever more deeply into the ocean of our salvation.

God used a man named William Wilberforce to abolish the slave trade in Great Britain. A contemporary, John Newton, had been a slave trader during the same era before God changed his heart.

Their friendship and co-laboring to abolish slavery is documented in the film *Amazing Grace*. In it, Wilberforce asks Newton to write down the record of all he remembers from his days as a slave trader. Newton balks, replying that there were twenty thousand ghosts that haunted him and he just could not write it down—it was too painful. But just as the abolition decision was about to occur in Parliament, God changed Newton's heart, and Newton boasted deeply in the amazing grace he wrote about. He allowed it to really seep into the pores of his soul. So Newton set his mind to do what his friend asked of him and to document and face the twenty thousand ghosts. He sat down and wrote everything he remembered—every cry, every scream, every instance of torture, every face, every mother, every child, every father, every family separated. In the film, as he is drudging the recesses of his horrific memories, William Wilberforce appears and Newton begins to weep, crying over his sin for the first time.

"Here it is," he says, "the record of the twenty thousand ghosts." What follows is the crux of all of repentance. "I am old, but I've learned two things. That I am a very great sinner. And Jesus Christ is a very great Savior."

John Newton boasted in a big Savior because he needed a big Savior. He now saw he was a big sinner. When Newton was able to write down and really experience what his sin had cost so many—God, others, and himself—he was finally able to truly grieve it. The connection is meaningful to us today: Newton was not able to weep until he wrote down the specifics of his sin and the cost of his sin to himself and to others.

Newton's story begs the question of us: when was the last time we wept over sin? Do we trust big grace to allow us to sit and enumerate our need, just as Newton did? We cannot manufacture this type of grief. We cannot create the purity of the gift of grace that tears of repentance would bring to us. May God grant us hearts that are so sensitive to the Spirit that we would mourn and repent over our sin when needed. May God grant us the grace to face our own twenty thousand ghosts, knowing his power and strength will enable us to leave the encounter as changed people, more reflective of his Son.

Useful Grief, Useful Law

We arrive at godly grief that draws our hearts to repentance through intimate knowledge of God's heart through God's Word. It is God's law that exposes our hearts, showing us it is not just a little bit of difference between us and God, but rather an insurmountable chasm of distinction between us in character and motivation. We may be more familiar with the concept of the law being useful and helpful, or how God calls Spirit-filled Christians to make commitments to and resolve to follow after Christ in obedience (known by theologians as the Third or Reformed Use of the Law), but we may be less familiar with the another use of the law, which is to lead us to repentance (known by theologians as the Second or Lutheran Use of the Law). God's law exposes sin so that we are humbled and broken by it. From this humble, broken place we see our helplessness, and we are driven to Christ, as we see in Galatians 3:19–24. God's law drives us to despair of self so that we would have no other recourse than to look afresh upon Jesus.

Humility and helplessness may make us feel squeamish or even downright exposed, so much so that our flesh may want to fight against allowing the Word to slay us. We think, "That's what causes depressed Christians!" Actually, just the opposite is the case. Humility and helplessness do not cause depressed Christians. Depressed Christians think God loves them more if they have obeyed his Word and that he will love them less and bless them less if they disobey. That is why they get depressed. These Christians are all around us—you may even identify yourself as one—and they are so frustrated because they think God's main concern is them getting their act together. Carrying the weight of getting your act together before an infinitely holy God will undoubtedly make you anxious to get things right; it will inevitably make you depressed.

But when we understand the grace, mercy, and love of God, and the incredible identity we have been given in Christ through the gift of his righteousness, and that because of Christ's work God now delights in us at all times (Zeph. 3:17)—simply put, we will be changed in heart and action. We can hold in tension that God does not delight in our sin, but that he is able to distinguish between our sinful thoughts, attitudes, motives, and behaviors on the one hand, and us as persons united to Christ on the other hand. And we as people who are righteous in Christ? Well, God always delights in us! Isn't that amazing? Every believer in Jesus Christ must live in this tension. In our persons united to Christ, we are completely pleasing to God. But in our daily condition as it relates to the truth of God's Word, all of our thoughts, words, deeds, attitudes, motives, and actions are either objectively pleasing to God or displeasing (1 Thess. 2:4;

4:1). This side of heaven we will only begin to plumb the depths of the significance of this truth. A safe place to start is to soak in the steady safety of always being able to go to God in repentance. We need never fear he is going to backhand us. The Christian who feels safest in the grip of grace is the Christian who is the quickest to truly repent.

My wife breeds and raises Golden Retrievers. You can learn a lot about the Christian life from raising dogs. One mistake people often make in training dogs is related to correction of bad behaviors. How many times has a dog misbehaved, you have called it to you in anger, and when it comes you discipline it? Congratulations, you have just trained your dog not to come when you call it. Why would it continue to run to you if it knows you are going to discipline it when it comes? No, you discipline a dog in the act of misbehaving, but never when it responds to you. If we feel God will meet us with a slap when we turn to him in repentance, we will be slow in coming home. But, if we know he waits for us like the prodigal's father waited for him in love, then we will more quickly come home to love in repentance.

The Christian who feels safest in the grip of grace is the Christian who is the quickest to truly repent.

In Max Lucado's book *No Wonder They Call Him the Savior*, Lucado shares the story of a young Brazilian girl named Christina who lived in a very poor town—a slum, really. Her mother's home had a wood burning stove, a dirt floor, and small mats on the floor where they would sleep. Christina longed to escape the harsh realities of her home for the excitement and glitz of city life. One night while her family was asleep, she left for the big city. When her family awoke the next morning her mother, Maria's, heart was broken. Having grown up in the slum herself, Maria was a lot more street-wise than her daughter. She knew what awaited her daughter in the city.

Maria immediately booked a ticket for a bus to Rio de Janeiro. Just before she left, she went to a local drug store and spent all her remaining money on black and white photo booth photos. Behind that tiny drawn curtain, Maria took as many pictures of her face as her remaining money would allow. Maria boarded the bus to Rio and went directly to the worst sections of Rio's slums, where the streetwalkers and prostitutes might be found. At every place she visited, she tacked a picture of her face with the same note scrawled on the back. Finally, all her money was gone, Maria had to return home. She left dejected.

A few weeks later, Christina's dream had turned into a nightmare. As she descended the stairs of a hotel, sad and dejected herself, she noticed a familiar face tacked to a wall. Her throat began to tighten and she teared up as she recognized the picture of her mother. Christina removed the tack to examine the photo. As she turned it over in her hand she saw the note, "Whatever you have done, whatever you have become, it doesn't matter. Please come home."[13]

In Christ, the message is the same for us today. "No matter where you've been, no matter what you've done, come home." That is what the gospel means. We can always come home to love in repentance. But we must begin there—we must ask the Spirit to initiate repentance in our hearts. What we cannot do,

---

[13] Max Lucado, *No Wonder They Call Him the Savior* (Portland, OR: Multnomah, 1986), 158-9.

however, is live in denial, because that will mean we stay stuck in our sin forever. If God's going to do a work of grace and transformation in our lives, it is going to begin with an exposure of sin. It is going to begin with the first step of the Gospel Waltz: repentance.

What Are We Repenting Of?

I am constantly amazed at how readily my own heart can rationalize ungodly thoughts, attitudes, motives, and behaviors. We all do it. Many people live in a dream world of rationalization. Part of repentance is to stop playing mental games with ourselves and instead to acknowledge that sin is really sin. In Genesis 6:5 we see the widespread, all-encompassing nature of sin when it states that, "The LORD saw that the wickedness of man was great in the earth, and that every intention of the thoughts of his heart was *only evil continually.*"

This side of the cross, by grace the music does not end on a note of condemnation. A remarkable seminary professor and lover of global missions, Jack Miller, was likely the first to remark, "Cheer up, you're a lot worse than you think! But cheer up, God's grace is far better than you could ever imagine."[14] This professor found missionaries were typically waning on the mission field due to greatly underestimating their own brokenness and the wonder and beauty of divine grace. When their time on the field exposed it, they were so filled with shame and despair that they either left the field or stopped being bold and consistent in their witness. He helped the missionaries see that it

[14] Michael A. Graham, *Cheer Up! The Life and Ministry of Jack Miller* (Phillipsburg: P&R, 2020), 23.

was the fact of their sin that tempted them to lose heart but that they expected to be better than they were. They expected the fact that they were missionaries to lead them to be super saints. Missionary or homemaker, seminary professor or charter boat captain, we are all in desperate need of the grace of God, and we begin to taste and experience it through repentance.

When I am honest before the Father and allow the Holy Spirit to speak to me of my own sin, I am not proud to tell you the enumeration of sins can go on and on. Even Paul says in Galatians 5:21 "things like these." In other words, when it comes to the understanding of sin, we rarely do more than just scratch the surface. But what Paul is saying is: *There is right. There is wrong. And grace gives you the boldness and the strength to look at what is right and what is wrong and to use it as a mirror for your life. And if you are exposed you'll run to the cross of Christ, and you'll receive forgiveness and power to be changed.*

Turn from Sin

Perhaps my favorite illustration for sin comes directly from the Hebrew word for repent, *shub*, which means to turn. As we are encountering this paradigm of the Gospel Waltz as a means of tangibly abiding with Christ on a daily basis, how appropriate that the origins of the first step, Repent, are a dance move. To turn is to change the direction we are facing, perhaps to turn our back on an old partner and face a new one. When we turn our back to sin and face Christ, we will experience a partnership so sweet, so life-giving, and so fulfilling that we will begin to have a right view of our old partner and the destruction and harm it caused to ourselves and those around us. When we turn toward Christ, we are enabled to see our old partner clearly, acknowledge that sin is sin and that we are guilty of it. We are enabled to repent in the particulars and not just in general. We can examine our attitudes and motives, not just our behaviors, and expand the definition of sin which, in turn, greatly expands our experience of grace.

The Call to Repentance is the call to turn and find the most beautiful dance partner you could ever imagine—one who is ready to change you and take you on adventures you never could dream up on your own.

Yes, But How?

A gospel paradigm creates a safe place for people to acknowledge their sin, therefore cultivating a culture of repentance. As more and more Christians—especially the most mature—admit and confess their sins, a culture of repentance becomes the norm in a community. Repentances breeds repentance! We can see this practiced in the home, in the church, in friendships . . . everywhere. If people in a city know there is a church that actually practices authentic and honest repentance, they will beat a path to your door to become part of the fellowship. Unbelievers are drawn in when God's people aren't pretending to have it all together when they clearly don't.

If you find yourself unsure of what to repent of, I would like to suggest a simple exercise I often employ.[15] It involves simply listening to yourself. In Matthew 12:34 Jesus teaches that out of the abundance

---

[15] Jack Miller; *Sonship* (Jenkintown: World Harvest Mission, 1994), 36, 48.

of the heart the mouth speaks. We can practice this by listening to the words that flow most naturally out of our mouths. Are they defensive words? Are they words that tear others down so that we might feel more built up? Are they words of grumbling or complaining? Are they words that betray arrogance? Are they words of impatience? Identifying the type of words we find ourselves using can expose our hearts and reveal our need for repentance.

In Psalm 139:23–24 David asks God: "Search me O God, and know my heart. Try me and know my thoughts. See if there be any grievous way in me and lead me in the way everlasting." We, too, can make this our continual prayer: *Lord, search me, try me.* Expose grievous ways in me. In other words, we must pray for repentance and seek it in our prayer life. Repentance is a grace; it is something that is granted to us, not something we manufacture (Acts 11:18; 2 Tim. 2:25). If we find ourselves still unsure of what to repent of, we can repent of that! Before the Father we can even repent of a lack of awareness of the depths of our sin. We can seek after a repentant heart.

If you feel stuck here at the first step of the Waltz, a great place to start is with trusted friends. In safe community, a question to ask one another is whether or not we are growing in repentance. And if you look at each other without an answer, repent of that! If we were to sit down for coffee and I were to ask you what you have been repenting of these days, and you didn't have an answer, that is a pretty good indication that you are likely not making much progress in sanctification right now. Tell God you fear that you are not really growing. Then listen, watch, and wait for his ever-effective Spirit to move in your heart, drawing you in kindness toward the first step of the Gospel Waltz (Rom. 2:4).

When it comes to repentance, the ability to be honest with others in community or with God himself is based on our grasp of the love of God for us. Remember the illustration of the father throwing rocks at the little boy's boat? Remember the story of Christina from Brazil? When we understand God's love drops things into our lives so that the waves created will drive us back to his loving arms, we will be granted a right perspective on repentance. For a real return (literally, a re-turn) to take place, we need to be convinced of the love of God for us. Without the conviction that there is a loving God waiting for us, we will never return home.

Because all of God's anger and wrath for our sin was poured out upon Christ, God treats us not as our sins deserve, but as Christ's righteous life deserves to be treated. Just like Christina, we can always come home.

Repenting As Fast As We Can

Many years ago I led a ministry event overseas. It was a week of deep conversations, powerful conversions, impactful community with the global church, and opportunities to influence ministries and minds. While the work of God in the world was apparent all week long, the work of God in my own heart happened on the plane ride home, through the movie that was playing, of all things.

The movie was the star-studded Meryl Streep and Clint Eastwood film *Bridges of Madison County*. In the film, Streep and Eastwood begin an affair while her husband is out of town with the children. She is ready to leave her family for this new love, but at the last minute decides not to. Eastwood is quite confused, so Streep explains that though every little girl dreams of her wedding day and all her hopes coming true, the reality is that with marriage, many women realize they are willing to die to their own dreams to make those of their husband and children come true. Having remembered her commitment to her family, Streep says no to his invitation to leave town with her.

As the scene ended, I found tears streaming down my cheeks. I wept—bawled, actually—and took my feelings before the Lord. While I thought I was just innocently watching a movie on a plane, God had other plans. He used the plot to unearth a dark reality in my own heart. Similar to the plot of the movie I, too, was having an affair, and my mistress was ministry—the Bride of Christ.

In the minutes of watching scenes of other loves unfold, I realized that I had left my wife, my sweet love, home alone managing three children under five. And it was not just this trip. This was a continual practice; it was a lifestyle of making ministry my mistress. Over and over I had turned to my wife and said, "Sweetheart, the kingdom calls. I've got to go."

It hit me at thirty thousand feet somewhere over the Atlantic that my dear wife Laurie had died to all her dreams so that she could facilitate the fulfillment of mine. I was cut to the heart.

Right then and there I took out a piece of paper and started repenting. I wrote down all the ways I failed to affirm her, how I assumed I could do what needed to be done without considering her needs, and how rarely I took into account her difficulties. I just wrote and wrote. I enumerated the ways I appreciated her and told her how sorry I was that I did not tell her more often.

I wrote pages and pages, my shame and guilt and exposure toppling right onto the paper.

Quickly, I stuffed the letter in an envelope and sealed it up tight before I could have a moment to think twice.

When I arrived home, embarrassment swarmed and I was too ashamed to give it to her. So I made up an excuse to go to the store. As I was heading out the door, I nearly tossed it at her as I said, "Here honey, read this." And I left.

I stayed away for about thirty minutes. At the time, we had a garage door that was attached to the kitchen, and I knew she could hear the garage door open as she was cooking dinner. Mustering the courage, I slunk up the stairs wondering what was going to meet me when I walked in. But when I walked through that door to my sweet bride, tears were streaming down her face. When I asked her what the tears were, she said through her sobs, "This makes me want to love you so much more than I do! I am so drawn to your vulnerability and honesty over your brokenness, and it makes me want to repent more as well!" I saw the truth play out in my own marriage: repentance really does breed repentance.

When Martin Luther nailed the 95 Theses to the door at Wittenberg, it was no coincidence that the first dealt with repentance. It is the quintessential part of the Christian life. Luther wrote, "When our Lord and Master Jesus Christ said 'Repent' (Matt. 4:17), he willed the entire life of believers to be one of repentance."[16] Not just for the start of it, but for the entire Christian life. We see this need for repentance in Christ's teaching (Mark 1:15), at Pentecost (Acts

---

[16] Martin Luther, *Ninety-Five Theses* (1517), 9.

2:38), and even in the first Beatitude (Matt. 5:3). Renewal, revival, restoration, transformation—it all begins with repentance, brokenness, contrition, and humility. There is something about repentance that truly melts the heart of God. God is moved by human repentance and confession of need and brokenness. Repentance is not a dirty word, it is not a shameful word. Repentance is actually the result of God pursuing our hearts through exposing them to show us our fresh need for the Savior. God just cannot resist moving in grace toward anyone who repents.

How We Repent

1. **Increasingly**: We will never "arrive" on this side of heaven. Our journey of sanctification will only serve to bring us into increasing awareness of the depths of our sin.
2. **Whole-Heartedly**: Repentance that changes us fully grieves the cost of sin to ourselves, others, and God. Plentiful repentance is a demonstration of plentiful love.
3. **Hopefully**: Repentance is based on our utter hope in Christ's completed work, not in our abilities.
4. **Expectantly**: Repentance is based on our reliance on the supernatural work of the Holy Spirit to transform our hearts and lead to the fruit of repentance.

Chapter 5 Summary

- Repentance is an invitation back into intimacy with God. But he never turned away; we did.
- God's kindness leads us to repentance.
- Godly grief produces a repentance that leads to salvation.

Reflection Questions

1. Is there an attitude that you are minimizing or excusing? Is there a behavior that you are trying to convince yourself is really not all that bad?
2. How are you filled with self-righteousness or self-indulgence?
3. How are you following what your flesh desperately wants, rather than submitting to the Word of God?
4. Is God calling you to repent over your lack of repentance?
5. Can you think of one or two trusted friends that you would like to have an honest conversation about repentance with?

6

BELIEVE: THE LEAST PRACTICED STEP

When Jesus tells us in Matthew 18:3 that "unless you turn and become like children, you will never enter the kingdom of heaven," I see a clear parallel to one of my favorite children's movies, as perhaps nothing better illustrates the *Believe* step of the Gospel Waltz better than *Toy Story*.

The film stars two friends who are toys: Woody the cowboy and Buzz Lightyear the space ranger astronaut action figure. We come to realize early on that Buzz thinks he is an actual space hero with true superpowers. Through crazy circumstances that only Pixar could concoct, Buzz *does* seem to fly, and Woody is unable to convince Buzz that he is just a toy.

In a time of crisis, Buzz's skills are put to the test and left wanting, as he comes to realize that Woody was right and he does not actually have superpowers. Buzz acknowledges he is just a toy and falls into despair and hopelessness. In perhaps one of the most quintessential Pixar moments, Woody reminds Buzz to check the sole of his space boot. And there, inked in a child's handwriting, is the name *Andy*. He is Andy's. Knowing all along that Buzz had no superpowers, but delighting in him all the same, Andy had lovingly marked Buzz as his own. A seemingly small detail holds the key to Buzz's entire purpose, and as Buzz reflects upon who he belongs to, he is filled with new determination.

The gospel works the same way as we preach it to ourselves. We are promised in Galatians 3:1–5, 2 Corinthians 3:18, and Romans 15:13 (among other places) that the physical, mental, emotional, and volitional act of believing in the gospel activates supernatural transforming power, both enabling us to experience deeper intimacy with the Father and empowering us to live renewed lives. Despite our wrong assertions that we are self-sufficient in our own power, God has eternally marked us as his people. Revelation 14:1 says that God's name will be written on the foreheads of those who know him. And even more radically, Isaiah 49:16 says that we are engraved on God's hands. He does not just mark us with his name—an unspeakable gift of identity in itself. He also marks himself with our names—at the very place that was pierced for our transgressions. What an unbelievable reality! And yet believing the unbelievable is precisely what he asks of us (Eph. 3:18–19).

We saw earlier that in John 6 the Jews asked Jesus what they needed to do in order to do the works of God. He answered them succinctly in verse 29: "This is the work of God: to believe in the one he has sent." While his answer is plain, almost nothing could have been more difficult for their hearts to comprehend, and I would offer that nothing remains more difficult for our modern hearts to grasp. The one work—the one thing above all else we are called to do as Christ followers—is to believe. And what is it that we are to believe? The unbelievable: that our identity is not found in what we do but in what has been done for us.[17]

> How are you righteous before God?
>
> Only by true faith in Jesus Christ. Even though my conscience accuses me of having grievously sinned against all God's commandments, of never having kept any of them, and of still being inclined toward all evil, nevertheless, without any merit of my own, out of sheer grace, God grants and credits to me the perfect satisfaction, righteousness, and holiness of Christ, as if I had never sinned nor been a sinner, and as if I had been as perfectly obedient as Christ was obedient for me. All I need to do is accept this gift with a believing heart. (Heidelberg Catechism Question 60, 1563)

Do yourself a favor. Read those words again. Reflect on them, savor them, and believe them. They are life-changing words.

Faith Is Not the Absence of Doubt

Lots of people talk about faith, but what is it? Some faith traditions offer that it is some subjective experience that we are all supposed to have that makes us feel close to God. Others suggest it is the absence of doubt—an absolute certainty that never wavers. Common phraseology may suggest it is something we muster up, regulate, or borrow, as we toss around

---

[17] Randal Working *From Rebellion to Redemption* (Colorado Springs: NavPress, 2001), 133.

phrases like, "She has a lot of faith." I would like to offer us a working definition that I hope will help:

> The word "faith" describes the human activity of doing nothing except receiving and resting upon a promise given to us by God.

Similarly, J. I. Packer, who famously wrote *Knowing God*, says, "Faith is not the ground of justification. It is rather the empty hand that by receiving Christ, receives righteousness."[18] In other words, Faith is simply the empty hand which receives the promises of God.

When we believe the truth of the gospel concerning our identity in Christ when we least feel we deserve it, the transforming power of grace is activated in deeper measure in our lives.

Faith, like humility, is actually an *anti*-work. It is precisely the place for feeling incompetent! Because if you feel incompetent, it actually qualifies you to be a person of faith. Faith simply looks away from itself in its need to the great Need-Meeter. When we believe the truth of the gospel concerning our identity in Christ when we least feel we deserve it, the transforming power of grace is activated in deeper measure in our lives (2 Cor. 3:18).

We, as believers in Jesus, must be told over and over and over again that the voices we hear do not dictate or define our reality. We have to be willing to step outside of our experience and believe in the realities and promises of the Word of God. This is why we read in Psalm 42:5 that David takes hold of himself and says, "Soul, hope in God!" It is also why Paul calls us

---

[18] J.I. Packer; *18 Words: The Most Important Words You Will Ever Know* (Geanies House: Christian Focus, 2007), 135–42.

to take every thought captive to the obedience of Christ (2 Cor. 10:3–6). Faith is not the absence of sin or the complete silencing of the voices telling us just how badly we have failed or the presence of doubts big or small. Struggling against sin and doubt does not minimize the existence of true faith within our soul. Faith is simply the presence of a mustard seed of itself. When we step outside of our experience to believe God's Word rather than our experience, we are not being hypocritical or fake—we are actually living by faith!

Late one evening my son, Josh, was in high school and was supposed to be studying for one of his finals. I walked into our basement to find him playing computer games. My mind can jump from point A to point Z rather quickly, but that day it traveled at lightning speed. Before I could even open my mouth to ask Josh if there might be something else he was supposed to be doing, my brain was sending images of Josh standing in the unemployment line.

With that image in mind, I forewent a fatherly question and went straight to a verbal bashing: *How did he think he would do well on a final if he was wasting his time playing video games? Had he even thought about his future?* When I was finally silent, Josh's eyes were down and streaming with tears.

I felt awful—not just because I had gone from zero to 120 in five seconds, but also because I was parenting from fear.

I talked to him and tried to make it better. Then I left to get ready for bed and tried talking to myself to make it better. Nothing was working as I climbed into bed and said to my wife, "Honey, I need you to pray for me. I just feel like a total failure. I think I'm so worried about my son not turning out alright that I may be the reason he doesn't turn out alright."

Laurie dropped her book and propped herself up on her elbow, looking me straight in the eyes. "Well," she began, "it sounds to me like you're really going to have to believe this grace stuff you teach us all the time."

And just like that, I was mercifully undone.

My wife was right. In kindness, she asked me questions that helped me see how I was falling back into old patterns and wanting to build my own record of righteousness again. She reminded me I have no record of my own doing to stand on, and I have no choice but to depend on someone else's. She reminded me of what I preach to others every Sunday, that faith comes down to depending entirely on the perfect, wonderful, righteous, just, and kind Jesus. Keeping the object of our faith in sight not only saves us from hell, but also gives us a sense of our daily acceptance and the moment-by-moment delight of Father God over us and the ability to enter confidently into repentance and rest—not if, but when we need to.

Yes, But How Do We *Do* This 'Believe' Thing?

And here is the hitch; it's the part that trips many of us up, especially those of us who struggle with a try-harder mentality. When it comes to the daily work of abiding in Christ, we likely know fairly well how to repent, but just how do we engage in the anti-work of belief?

The Gospel Waltz offers some practical help as we approach this second step, and it will serve us to consider this step in two parts.

1. **Affirm** the truths of the gospel regarding our identity in Christ, then
2. **Appropriate** the truths of the gospel regarding our transformation in Christ.

Let's take a closer look at these two elements of the Believe step of the Waltz.

Part I: Affirm

Affirm Our Justified Standing

Through faith in Christ we are declared righteous before God—justified: *just-as-if-I'd never sinned* and *just-as-if-I'd always and ever only done everything right.* As a pastor, I say that line a lot. In fact, I have to remind myself to step back from it and be awed by the realities of it once again. It is so easy for it to roll off my lips and far more challenging for me to really believe.

Paul declares in Philippians 3:9 that his aim in life is to live moment by moment according to his justified standing and be found in Christ, "not having a righteousness of [his] own that comes from the law, but that which comes through faith in Christ." This is true of us because by grace through faith, the Holy Spirit has baptized us into union with Christ. We have been ushered into a standing of righteousness before God the Father, which means his unchanging delight and his unending favor are upon us right now.

Having God's love, delight, and favor has absolutely nothing to do with earning it or deserving it.

And it has absolutely nothing to do with what we do.

That is hard to swallow, isn't it? Having God's love, delight, and favor has absolutely nothing to do with earning it or deserving it. Because we are justified by grace through faith in Jesus Christ, there is nothing we could ever do that could make God love us more than he already does. And because we are justified by grace through faith in Jesus Christ, there is nothing we could ever do that could cause God to ever decrease his love for us.

One evening in our newcomer's small group as I was covering the difference between the gospel paradigm and the works paradigm, I explained that grace does not mean God rejoices over our sin, but somehow, in our person being united to Christ, God is always rejoicing over us.

When we got to this portion of the discussion, a young woman named Maria became visibly upset. Tears began to stream down her face from a sincerely tender place. I stopped my explanation and asked Maria if she could voice what was behind her tears. As she composed herself, waving her hand in front of her eyes in a futile attempt to dry them, she stammered, "This . . . This is . . . This just seems too good to be true. I've never heard it like this." She got it exactly right. Because it does seem to be too good to be true, doesn't it? That is why it is called good news.

Each person in the group grew teary-eyed as we entered into Maria's awe and joy. We rejoiced not just for Maria's newfound understanding, but for ourselves as well as we experienced the gospel of grace afresh in our own lives. Maria's transparency in processing the gospel made the good news become good to all of us all over again.

It is this wondrous love that I must preach to my own heart over and over again until I believe it afresh. It is also a love we must continually preach to one another, just as my wife did with me propped up on her elbow, probably wondering if her pastor-husband really believed his own words. This act of preaching the gospel both to ourselves and to others is a habit we must cultivate in order to remember what is true because our hearts are like Teflon, and the gospel continually slips off.[19]

What Is Justification?

Justification is a legal term. It takes place in the courtroom of God, and God the Father is the judge. Our prosecutor may be Satan (Rev. 12:10 refers to him as our accuser), but oftentimes this prosecutor does not even need to whisper in our ears for us to feel guilt. Our consciences are guilty enough, and they can be relied upon to accuse us, as we see all the way back in Genesis 3. We find ourselves firmly in the seat of the defendant, and Christ himself is the defense attorney. We have all kinds of evidence against us, and Satan proceeds to open the files and present the case. There is no escaping as it is all aired—every unkind, ungodly, unloving thought, every motive that was not God-centered or Christ-oriented. Every deed that goes against God's law, not to mention every deed we fail to do that God's law tells us to do—it is all recorded. Satan has perfect recollection, and the evidence is abundant. There is no denying it—it is all true.

God hears the evidence, picks up his gavel, and declares the verdict: *not guilty.*

"Objection your honor!" Satan is out of his chair. "How can you do that? You've just taken a perfect outlaw and declared them to be a model citizen. You cannot do that."

Not guilty.

"Objection your honor! You are ignoring the evidence!"

---

[19] Jerry Bridges, *The Discipline of Grace* (Colorado Springs: NavPress, 1994), 46.

And God speaks to silence the accuser: *No, I am not ignoring the evidence. I acknowledge the evidence. I am acquitting the guilty and declaring them a model citizen, perfectly obedient to every law.*

In effect, God himself—as Judge—climbs down from the bench and with his own hands places his Son in the defendant's seat. God presents the evidence of the perfect obedience of Christ and asks if there is any evidence to the contrary. *Crickets.* In spite of the silence, in spite of the evidence of Christ's perfect life, God pronounces Jesus guilty and proclaims the punishment: gruesome death. Do we get this? Do we really get this? Our sin and guilt and punishment were imputed to Jesus, the perfect One. His righteousness, obedience, and sonship was imputed to us, the actual guilty party. God then decrees that his people in Christ are not just not guilty but also declared innocent, as if they had never broken any law and in fact kept all of them perfectly. Christ has borne the burden and punishment of the sin. The gavel drops. Case closed.

But, But, But . . .

The problem is, we don't believe it, do we? Most of us would never deny our need to be saved by justification by grace through faith. But we have relegated justification to the moment of conversion, and we have begun to teach ourselves and our consciences, "Yes, I am justified by grace through faith, and when I die and I appear before the judgment seat of God he is going to declare me not guilty, and I am going to be able to get into heaven." We have truncated the magnitude of justification. It is far more than just a "Get Out of Hell Free" card.

Justification cannot be a doctrine we just put up on a shelf after conversion. It is not something we pull into conversations to impress people with how we can wield fancy theological concepts. Never. This is truth to warm our soul, rock our world, shake us from our complacency, and impact our lives every day. If we are in Christ, God delights in us and pours out his favor upon us completely divorced from anything we do or do not do. (If you feel I just went too far, consider the alternative. How would you ever know if you are living in God's favor or not if it depended upon what you do? Considering the two great sins of omission and commission, how would you ever know if you've done enough?). In Christ, God justifies the ungodly (Rom. 4:5). God simply declares us righteous. It is not something he does *in* us. It is not something he does *to* us. It is something he declares to be true *of* us. Even our level of comprehension is of no consequence—its truth does not depend on our grasp of it. Our *experience* of this truth, however, is impacted by whether we believe it on a moment by moment basis or not. Sometimes we grow in our experience of a truth when we better understand the component parts of that truth. So let's dig a little deeper still.

Justification cannot be a doctrine we just put up on a shelf after conversion. This is truth to warm our soul, rock our world, shake us from our complacency, and impact our lives every day.

The Doctrine of Justification through the Ages

The gospel that Martin Luther believed, taught, and risked his life for is about what is termed by theologians as *passive righteousness*. His understanding of Scripture stood in stark contrast to the teachings of the sixteenth century church—the false gospel of works for the daily Christian life that my own try-harder heart wants to pull me back toward even four centuries later. Luther's revelation was straight from Scripture, and it revealed a righteousness that we don't (and cant'!) lift a finger to attain. This righteousness is the direct result of the obedience performed for us by another, and that another is Jesus.

Frequently I ask the unchurched or those new to our church what is the first thing they think of when they think of Jesus. Without fail, people answer that they think of the crucifixion, which is, of course, a most vital component of our faith. Theologians refer to this as the *passive obedience* of Christ taking on God's wrath as he simply hung on the cross. But Christ merely *dying* to take away our sins is not the story in full. Christ *living* every moment of his entire life in perfect obedience and fulfilling the law is just as much of a vital part of the story. Theologians refer to this as the *active obedience* of Christ—his active fulfillment of the law on our behalf. This radical, mind-blowingly perfect obedience was not solely to please the Father; he was doing it on our behalf. Jesus obeyed for *me*. Jesus obeyed for *you*. So, putting it all together: the passive and active obedience of Christ is what leads to the passive righteousness of the believer, which is a righteousness we cannot lift a finger to attain. If we grasp this truth in the core of our being, it will change our lives.

Charles Dickens' masterful and sweeping novel *A Tale of Two Cities* tells the story of two men from two vastly different backgrounds who bear a striking physical resemblance and are both in love with the same woman. Set during the build up toward the

French Revolution and the Reign of Terror, the resemblance of the two men, Charles Darnay and Sydney Carton, becomes pivotal as Charles Darnay is set to hang for his aristocratic lineage.

In perhaps the most poignant and heroic example of fictional substitutionary death, Sydney Carton changes places with Darnay—swapping identity down to the prisoner's ragged clothing off his back—to be carried away in place of Darnay. "It is a far, far better thing that I do than I have ever done;" Carton says at the end of his life, "it is a far, far better rest that I go to than I have ever known." Because of Sydney Carton's sacrifice, another person was able to experience fullness of life.

But the most striking resemblance is not actually between the physical appearance of Dickens' characters. The real beauty of the story lies in the resemblance to Christ's substitutionary death in our place. And true to the gospel narrative, the real story is actually even better than Dickens' shadow, as Christ did not just die in our place, but also took on our humanity and lived in our place. He dressed himself in far more than a prisoner's rags. He became fully like us, "like his brothers in every respect," to complete the perfect living we could never muster, die the guiltless death none of us could have accomplished, and attain for us the peace with God we could never have gained for ourselves (Heb. 2:17; Rom. 5:1).

Right Belief Precedes Holy Living

The doctrinal standard for my specific denomination is the Westminster Confession of Faith. A smaller version is called the Westminster Shorter Catechism (initially written to teach the faith to children), and we used it as a family with our own growing children.

Question number three asks: *What do the scriptures principally teach?* The answer: *The scriptures principally teach what man is to believe concerning God, and what duty God requires of man.* We as the church across many denominations memorize that tenet—we teach it to our children, we recite it over and over, and still we can miss the entire point. The order of operations here is crucial. *What we believe has priority over what we do.* The Bible primarily is not about what we do. We have often gotten it all backwards in American evangelicalism.

Just as we saw with the marking on the bottom of Buzz Lightyear's boot, the principle is this: what you believe determines who you are and what you do. Belief precedes behavior, and right behavior is always preceded by right belief. By far, none of the churches Paul visited were as entrenched in sin and lawlessness as Corinth, but Paul could look at their church and *still give thanks* because they were still preaching the gospel of grace. Conversely, the only churches Paul never gives thanks for are the Galatian churches of southern Turkey. Rather, in that case, he launches straight into fiery rebuke for distorting the gospel of Christ (Gal. 1:6–9). Paul understood that even though the Corinthians' behavior was sideways and backward and downright messed up, if they kept on preaching and believing the gospel of grace, Grace would change their lives. Grace would lead them to repentance. Grace would lead them to new desires. Grace would lead them to changed behaviors.

Is your skin prickling a little? Do you have a little voice warning you that if people think they are justified freely every moment of their lives that they will start doing whatever they want? You are not alone in your fear that by elevating grace we minimize behavior, but it is actually the opposite: nothing calls us further into godly living than grasping more fully every day God's amazing grace. I have yet to hear, "Bob, I am so glad you taught me about justification, because I am going to get smashed tonight." Or, "I am so glad you taught me about justification, because I am going to leave my wife." No, that is absurd! "Are we to continue in sin that grace may abound? By no means!" (Rom. 6:1–2). Remember, it is not just the concept of justification understood that we are talking about; it is the promise of justification believed that actually activates supernatural power from heaven. If grace was just a concept to be assented to, abuse would be everywhere. But the power of grace is released as Christ is trusted.

Much of the initial spark of the Reformation can be credited to the apocryphal event of a significant debate between the contemporary theologians Erasmus and Martin Luther. Erasmus believed grace was like two parents on either side of a child, coaxing the child to use their own power to stand and walk. He argued the power was in being coaxed by love—in the mere thought of it—motivating us to act in response to the outside force of a parent's love.

Luther argued if only it was the case that we could be compared to a precious child, but we are actually far worse off than that; we are a helpless caterpillar in a ring of fire. And rather than seeing two loving caterpillar parents on either side of us, moving our spirits with their motivating caterpillar words, the only thing we see is a perilous situation. Luther argued when we look around we see an encompassing and overwhelming ring of fire encircling us. We are threatened on every side by the insurmountable wall of unbearable heat. There is no escape. We are doomed. Our only hope is in being plucked out of the ring. Help must come from above.

Sometimes it helps to look at the opposite side of the argument. Rather than asking how God's favor despite our behavior leads to obedience, let's ask what *not* believing in his favor leads to. Believing that God is *against* us because of our disobedience leads to discouragement, despair, and hopelessness. To carry it further, what does despair, etc., lead to? A search for something to numb the pain. And then? Opening ourselves up to all kinds of sin in a desperate attempt to take the edge off. So, if believing God is against us leads to all kinds of sin, then believing he is for us leads us to all kinds of righteous desires. And that is just on a rational level. Remember, we are not talking about mere concepts but about supernatural power.

Contrary to popular opinion, nothing will lead to holiness and godliness more than a deep trust and rest that we are declared righteous in the sight of God, permanently and forever, in spite of our failures. When we rest in Christ's righteousness and trust in our justification, that is the faith that releases and activates the supernatural, transforming power of the Holy Spirit in our lives.

Affirm Our Adopted Status

In receiving grace, we not only affirm our justification each day of our lives, but we also affirm our adoption. When we choose to believe in, hope in, and rest in our justified standing when we least feel we deserve to, that is the point where the Holy Spirit fills us with the resurrection power of Christ. "This is the work of God, that you believe in him whom he has sent" (John 6:29).

In his classic book *Knowing God*, J.I. Packer answers one of the most important questions related to the issue of belief: *What is a Christian?*

> The richest answer I know is that a Christian is one who has God as Father. If you want to judge how well a person understands Christianity, find out how much he makes of the thought of being God's child, and having God as his Father. If this is not the thought that prompts and controls his worship and prayers and his whole outlook on life, it means that he doesn't understand Christianity very well at all. Our understanding of Christianity cannot be better than our grasp of adoption.[20]

Like justification, much of our daily experience of the benefits of the gospel depends on our heart's grasp of our adoption in Christ. And like justification, adoption also occurs in the courtroom of God. God, the Judge, signs the adoption papers and takes us into his family, treating us as Jesus himself, as the eternal Son. We have been given the standing of a brother or sister of Christ himself. We have been given the status of a daughter or son of God, and God has committed his love to us for eternity and sealed it with the completed work of Christ. The radical truth is that through the gospel, God the Father loves you and me *as much as* he loves Christ himself (John 17:23).

Just like justification, adoption does not change our heart or our nature, rather it is a declaration made by God about us. We do not earn it—we cannot. That is as ridiculous of a concept as the thought of a

---

[20] J.I. Packer, *Knowing God* (Downers Grove: InterVarsity Press, 1993), 200–01.

days-old baby behaving in some way so as to earn the favor of their adoptive parents—it just cannot happen. The decision is made apart from them, on their behalf, regardless of anything they have done or not done. I love how my friend and fellow pastor Monte Starkes puts it: "The only thing I have to contribute to my salvation is the sin that makes it necessary."

One of the best diagnostics to test how well we understand and are living in light of our adoption in Christ is to look deeply at an astounding passage hidden in one of the Old Testament minor prophets, Zephaniah.

Zephaniah 3:17 says this:

> The LORD your God is in your midst,
> a mighty one who will save;
> he will rejoice over you with gladness;
> he will quiet you by his love;
> he will exult over you with loud singing."

Time for a pop quiz, and I hope you can answer honestly in your heart:

When do you feel that this verse is most true of you?
When do you most struggle to believe that this verse could be true of you?
When do you feel God stops singing or rejoicing over you?
When does he stop wanting to quiet you with his love?
When does he stop delighting in you?

If you can think of a single instance when Zephaniah 3:17 is not true of you, then it means you are looking to your own effort and record-building instead of Christ's completed, sure record of perfection to deem you worthy. If there is something that we have done or not done that can change God's delight in us, then we are believing that our sin affects whether or not God, our adoptive Father, rejoices over us. And if our sin in fact stops God from singing over us, then we are without hope because there is never a moment when we are not shot through with sin.

Even our tears of repentance must be plunged beneath the blood of the Lamb. Now, do not think for a moment that God ever delights in our sin. He hates our sin and has poured out his wrath upon Christ for it. But our persons, united to Christ, bring God's song of delight and rejoicing. Neither should we think that we cannot strive to live a life pleasing to God, as Scripture clearly says we can and we must. We will address this fully when we arrive at the Fight step of the Waltz.

Praise God that his drawing near, saving, rejoicing, quieting, loving, and singing over us does not depend on our behavior *at all.* Zephaniah 3:17 is true for the Christian. At all times. Even our least deserving moments. Period.

Affirming truths like Zephaniah 3:17 does not mean a mindless mantra or positive self-talk. To affirm something is to repeat it, profess it, testify to it, pronounce it, certify it, and attest to it. It is the confidence of a child of God to remind our souls of our unchanging status as beloved heirs with full rights, privileges, resources, and every spiritual blessing in the heavenly realms (Eph. 1:3; Rom. 8:17). As J. I. Packer says, "I am a child of God, and God is my father. Say that to yourself over and over and over again. Say it first thing in the morning, and last thing at night. As you wait for the bus, any time your mind is free, ask that you may be enabled to live as one who knows that it is all utterly and completely true." Intellectually assenting to and emotionally accepting this extraordinary love cannot help but change us from the inside out. God has designed the power of the gospel to work this way.

Part II: Appropriate

I've been told by professional dancers that in the Waltz there is actually a small pause in the middle of the second step. We have all heard of the Waltz as "One, Two, Three. One, Two, Three. One, Two, Three." But these dancers tell me it more accurately goes like this: "One, Two AND Three. One, Two AND Three. One, Two AND Three." There is a slight pause in Step Two. There is also a slight pause in the Believe Step of the Gospel Waltz, because there are two elements to the step: Affirm and Appropriate. Once we've affirmed our identity in Christ, we need to pause before we move on to the Fight step because of this second element to the Believe step: appropriate.

Once we are settled on the *what* of our belief (as we saw with the affirm element of the Believe step), it is time to turn to the *how*. We must now investigate exactly how we appropriate the power of transforming grace by faith, applying both grace and gospel to daily living.

As we trust in Christ, as we rest in our justification, as we rely upon God's adoptive declaration of us, the inner cynic comes out and we confess it is just so hard for us to believe it is going to change us. Sure my justification is guaranteed and my adoption is certain, but . . .

Is it going to help me love my spouse better?
Is it going to help me be a better father, a kinder roommate, a more loyal and honest friend?
Is it going to help me at work and in my vocation?
Is it going to help me with my finances?
Is it going to help me be a better Christian in the church?
In other words, how can believing and affirming my justification and adoption actually change me?

Let's go back to Numbers 21. Did believing God's promise regarding snake bites accomplish any real change in the lives of the people who looked at the bronze serpent in faith? It did. Real venom coursing through veins was neutralized. Faith worked! Change that was real and tangible was activated through faith in the promise of God, which he kept. There's a rub, though, isn't there? It was not their looking that healed them, but without looking they would not have been healed. It is a tension we still hold as believers, a mystery we will not understand fully until heaven. But if we can grasp the supernatural fruit of faith in the wilderness of Numbers 21, then we can grasp the hope today of the power of the gospel working in our lives to release us from the coursing venom of jealousy, impatience, anger, bitterness, greed, worry, or fear. When we participate in the same look of faith the Israelites took in Numbers 21, God activates and releases supernatural, transforming grace from heaven into our lives here and now. Grace is not simply a concept to affirm, but a reality to grow in, apply, and allow to change all areas of life.

But even if we know that we can do absolutely nothing to save ourselves, then the question remains: *Why is it often harder to believe that faith can change us than it is to believe that faith has saved us?*

Lay Hold of Christ in Us

It is never a good thing when the phone rings late at night. This night confirmed that, as the voice on the other end of the phone asked my wife Laurie, "Do you have a student at Belmont University named Michael Flayhart?" and then, "You need to get here as soon as you can. He's been struck by a car." Laurie and I sped straight to Vanderbilt's trauma center, making the middle of the night drive from Birmingham to Nashville in record time despite feeling as though every passing minute of that long drive had swollen to an hour. We had to get to our boy.

The immediate impact from Michael's traumatic injuries from the razor scooter accident gutted Laurie and I emotionally. As I sat beside him in Vanderbilt's Level 1 trauma center ICU in the coming hours and days, and then in the recovery rooms during hours of painful rehab, I have never wanted more to be able to identify with another person—to meld with him in such a way that I could take on his physical pain, alleviate his suffering, and make the reality of his circumstances anything but what they were. I identified with a new level of grief I had never previously experienced because it was my son, and I could not help him.

When we, as believers united to Jesus, use the words "Christ in us" or "us in Christ," they sound so sweet, so sanitized, so tidy. But sitting in those hospital rooms gave me a bitter taste of the reality of what it takes for Christ to identify with us, embody us, and still want to be with us. This exchange is anything but a sanitized experience. Rather, this exchange smells of sacrificial blood. It sounds like the agony of the cross. It cries the tears that burn just like the tears of a father, bedside in his son's hospital room. In reality it is anything but a tidy exchange. And when we see it for what it is, we believe just a little deeper that the exchange was made on our behalf by a loving Father, who not only chose but planned, orchestrated, and instituted every single aspect of the life, death, and resurrection of Jesus (as well as every detail of our lives!) in such a way that we might know our status as beloved children can never be changed, diminished, or even strengthened.

Praise God, Michael made a full recovery. But I hope I never recover from being invited into a deeper place of understanding and identifying with what it took for Jesus to identify with us.

Only from a sure place of knowing that our status as beloved children cannot be changed, diminished, or even strengthened can we begin to see how *our experience* of our union with him can be fortified and increased. Just as the "Believe" step has two elements—affirm and appropriate—so our union with Christ has two elements: us in Christ and Christ in us. As we affirm our justified standing and adopted status, the Holy Spirit strengthens our experience of our living union with him as us in Christ; we are hidden in him. As we appropriate the present value of the blood of Christ, the Holy Spirit strengthens our experience of our living union with him as Christ in us; he is hidden in us. To further this both/and:

> *Belief is affirming our justified standing and adopted status, thus strengthening our experience of us in Christ.*

AND

> *Belief is appropriating the present-day value of*

Jesus's blood, which strengthens our experience of Christ in us.

The idea of appropriation is not a new one. In the Old Testament, God promised he was going to give his people the promised land. But they still had to go in and lay hold of it—they still had to appropriate it. In fact, as we will see in the third step of the Waltz, they had to fight to appropriate that which was promised. In the same way, we fight the fight of faith, as Paul called it in 1 Timothy 6:12. And as Christians we must be willing to engage in the same seemingly paradoxical effort of belief.[21] But having every good thing promised to us in Christ, it is worth the effort of fighting to lay hold and take possession of that which has already been promised to us.

Appropriate Christ's Completed Work

In affirming our gospel identity and position, we remind ourselves of justification and adoption. In appropriating the gospel, we remind ourselves about the theological truth of sanctification. The Westminster Shorter Catechism defines sanctification as the work of God's free grace by which we are renewed in our whole person in the image of God and by which we are enabled more and more to die to sin and live to righteousness (Question 35).

---

[21] A look back in church history reveals that the saints of old grasped this. Think of two old hymns in particular: The Old Rugged Cross and Rock of Ages:

> The Old Rugged Cross—stained with blood so divine; a wondrous beauty I see. / 'Twas on that old cross, Jesus suffered and died to pardon and sanctify me.
>
> Rock of Ages—Let the water and the blood; from Thy wounded side which flowed; / Be of sin the double-cure, cleanse me from its guilt and power.

The Reformation, the greatest life-altering and world-changing revival since Pentecost, was not merely about justification by grace through faith. The reformation was also about sanctification by grace through faith.

Christ's death on the cross does not merely free us immediately from sin's penalty. His death also frees us continually and progressively from sin's power (and one day we will be completely free from sin's presence). Unfortunately for us, progressive freedom from sin's power is not automatic. We need to appropriate the benefits of the cross—like regular withdrawals from an infinite bank account—through the act of belief.

Appropriate the Power of the Holy Spirit

As we consider the Gospel Waltz, we should be reminded that we are really just presenting another way to think about what it means to abide in Christ; or what it means to be filled with the Spirit or how to walk in the Spirit. How do you know that you are filled with the Spirit right now? How do you know if you are walking in the Spirit? We use these terms all the time, but do we truly understand them and apply them?

Perhaps no passage is more direct on the present power of the Holy Spirit than Galatians 3:1–7. With an air of absolute bewilderment, Paul asks the Galatian church, "Who has bewitched you? . . . Having begun by the Spirit, are you now being perfected by the flesh?" This is basically the biblical equivalent of ESPN commentator Keyshawn Johnson's trademark, "c'mon man." *Did you really think you would start one way and then switch midway to a whole different paradigm, now entirely based on your work instead of God's power? Did you really think God would leave you to your own efforts? Did you go back to thinking that a walk with Christ was a self-reformation project?* I don't know about you, but I can feel the head shake.

The verb "crucified" is in the perfect tense in Galatians 3:1. It means a past action with results continuing into the present and the future. In other words, the crucifixion of Christ and our resulting justification was a work that occurred in the past but still brings present benefits to all those living in him in the here and now. We simply must continue to return in faith to the benefits of the cross again and again.

Paul continues in verse 2, "Does he who supplies the Spirit to you and works miracles among you do so by works of the law, or by hearing with faith?" *C'mon man.* Nothing has changed. In the here and now, both to the Galatians and to us—the modern-day Gentiles—we are both justified by faith *and* sustained, empowered, driven, fortified, sanctified, and purified by faith.

When it comes to the here and now, just as Paul says, we can trust in the Holy Spirit's effectual work. We can know that he is moving in and through us, molding and shaping us to look more like the Son. Our job begins with appropriating the promise that it is happening. We must believe.

If only we had something tangible . . . a reminder for our sheep-like hearts that there is much supernatural work happening in us and through us as believers in Jesus. *If only* there were something we could experience regularly, with multiple senses, alongside one another in the body of Christ so that our communal faith might also be strengthened . . .

It's time to talk, and I mean *really* talk, about communion.

Feed on Christ

We don't talk about it enough, so we miss the power of a rather regular element of our Christian worship service—communion. The Lord's Supper essentially serves as a summary statement and physical illustration of the gospel. It reminds us that though we were dead in our sins, we are now also mysteriously and miraculously united with Christ and given life that keeps on producing life. Our spiritual transformation is not from our own goodness. We are changed *supernaturally* by a holy God who exists outside of ourselves, yet dwells in us by his Holy Spirit and is committed to changing us from the inside out. This sacrament of remembrance and transformation exults the gospel of God's amazing grace that it is Christ alone who changes us.

Each communion service is a tangible way to both recall truth and appropriate supernatural resources that lead to lasting spiritual change. When we eat the bread and drink the wine, we are remembering that Christ had to die for our sins, that he made a covenant with us that can never and will never be broken, and that he has cleansed us by his blood, making us righteous. We are reminding ourselves afresh of the gospel. But it is more than just remembering. When we engage in the physical act of eating the bread and drinking the wine, we experience a spiritual and supernatural abiding with Christ in which the Holy Spirit works to conform us to the very image of God as we come repentantly, partake believingly, and leave fightingly. We leave more like Christ, whether we feel it or not. It is not magical, but it is supernatural. Our participation in communion is far more than a mere memorial.

Beware Placing Limits on the Sacrament

In the classic hymn, "Would You Be Free From Your Burden Of Sin," we sing that there is "power, power, wonder-working power in the blood of the Lamb," but what do we mean? We usually mean that the blood of Christ is able to deliver a soul from the penalty of sin: hell. But so often we stop there. Somehow, after conversion, the message magically converts to, "Okay, Christian, God has changed you and now it's time for you to get busy. It is time for you to do this and not do that," and we continue to pile on the imperatives.

Many evangelical congregations spend a lot of study and preaching time in the latter half of Paul's epistles, which emphasize the gospel commands. But when we jump immediately to these imperatives, we can skip over what Paul tends to emphasize in the first half of his letters to churches of new believers—that is, the *gospel indicatives*, or the truths of who Christ is, what he has done, and who we are in him. Consider the books of Ephesians and Romans. Both Ephesians 1–3 and Romans 1–11 are heavy on the indicatives (truths about God), with the latter halves, Ephesians 4–6 and Romans 12–15, being heavy on the imperatives (gospel commands for us). Paul knew that only once all the indicatives were fully settled could he address how we ought to live out our new lives.

Just as the Christian will never stop needing to hear the gospel of grace alone by faith alone, the Christian will also never grow beyond needing to hear of the wonders of the sacrament of communion. Rather than limiting the power of the sacrament, what would it look like to magnify the ongoing value of it both in our own hearts and in our interactions with other believers? I know for me it would protect me from approaching the table thoughtlessly, casually, or callously.

A couple years ago I was at our denomination's General Assembly, and I was late for the Lord's Supper. Everywhere you turn at General Assembly there is an old friend from seminary or a fellow pastor you want to compliment on an article you saw of theirs online. In short, I was close to missing communion, and I thought there may be a chance I was not going to make it. A compulsion came over me such that I was fighting the urge to book it down the hall and tackle one of the elders serving the elements because I was so desperate and hungry for Christ. That is what the Lords' Supper ought to be: when we really see our sin and need and then we see our sin and need in contrast to the hope of the gospel, and when we really see that the spiritual presence and power of Jesus is offered to us in the Lord's Supper—well, it just might make us want to tackle the elders as they dispense the elements and say, "Give me Christ. I must have Christ."

While the celebration of the Lord's Supper is a sacrament reserved for public worship, we can still feed deeply on Christ and drink of him every moment of every day as we waltz. As we repent of our sin and look to Christ, we affirm our justified standing and adopted status, experience fresh forgiveness and grace, appropriate the supernatural resources of the risen Christ to change us and our desires and then, equipped with fresh joy and fresh power, step out in new obedience. In a sense, we are called to step into a continuous sacramental life.

Just as the look of faith by the Israelites toward the pole in Numbers 21 released supernatural power to neutralize venom, the look of faith through taking communion (like waltzing) releases transforming power so that we are in fact changed at that moment. As an act of faith, we receive it. And one way we can do so is to believe that it is actually in the process of happening in that very moment, regardless of how I feel or what I see. Our response to the gospel must constantly be like Mary, who says in Luke 1:38, "Be it done to me according to your word."

The Speed of Transformation

Change can seem so slow in coming, can't it? I'll have people say that the Waltz does not work because they are not seeing or feeling the change that happens when we abide in Christ. But seeing or feeling change are not requirements for change to happen, and that certainly doesn't mean they are not happening at all. It is far more likely that the drastic change desired by these folks simply is not happening on the timetable they would like. Our job is to believe that the change rooted in Christ is indeed occurring.

A friend sent me a video of professional dancers dancing the Viennese waltz at the World Games when they were held in our city, Birmingham, Alabama, in 2022. Watching the couples, I was struck by the seamlessness, flow, and beauty of their movements. These expert and practiced dancers seemed to cover so much distance so quickly. And it may be true that the very same could be said of us as well when we have waltzed with Christ for decades.

But it is likely that as we waltz we sometimes experience exactly the opposite. We do not seem to be covering much ground—we do not seem to be moving across the dance floor as quickly as we would like.

The steps are stunted, labored, or even painful. It can feel like we are slogging through quicksand rather than gliding the distance of a ballroom floor, held in the embrace of a skillful partner.

It can seem impossible to believe that as believers in Jesus, we are in the arms of a skillful partner when our circumstances shout anything but. But when we can waltz with him, when we can choose to keep our eyes locked in on his, we will realize he is guiding us across the dance floor after all, perhaps even more gracefully than we could ever imagine. Remember: waltzing will not fix you. Waltzing is simply how broken people with broken lives live in a broken world until Christ returns, yet all the while experiencing substantial and progressive transformation of heart and life.

Moving through Belief

We have spoken quite a lot about God's supernatural transforming power over the course of the Believe step, and perhaps you feel your dancing shoes ready to complete that step and follow it through all the way to the third step of the Gospel Waltz. But the truth is, only from a repentant heart that acknowledges God's lordship and our failure (Repent step) and a heart settled on his unconditional love for us and his supernatural, transforming power toward us (Believe step) can we healthfully move into the actionable Fight step.

Should your heart not be ready to move to this action step, I urge you to slow down. Wait for the Spirit to have you so certain of the forgiveness of your Father and his abundant love and pursuit for you that then you are ready to learn how to move out in faith to honor him with your actions. We must remember the wake-up call issued by the author of Hebrews, "Therefore, while the promise of entering his rest still stands, let us fear lest any of you should seem to have failed to reach it. For good news came to us just as to them, but the message they heard did not benefit them, because they were not united by faith with those who listened. For we who have believed enter that rest" (Heb. 4:1–3).

Chapter 6 Summary

- What you believe determines who you are and what you do.
- The act of believing in the gospel activates supernatural transforming power, both enabling us to experience deeper intimacy with the Father and empowering us to live renewed lives.
- Keeping the object of our faith in sight not only saves us from hell, but also gives us a sense of our daily acceptance, the moment-by-moment delight of Father God over us, and the ability to enter confidently into repentance and rest—not if, but when we need to.
- We engage in believing by affirming the truths of the gospel regarding our identity in Christ and then appropriating the truths of the gospel regarding our transformation in him.

Reflection Questions

1. In what area of your life do you need to hear the Father singing and rejoicing over you?
2. What is getting in the way of you believing that he does so continually?
3. What is one area of life where you would relish seeing tangible change as you appropriate the gospel?
4. What is one area of life where you struggle to believe there is change because you do not feel or see it as you wish you did?
5. How did the ideas about communion land for you?

7

FIGHT: NOW DO IT!

In Joshua 1, as the leadership mantle is passed from Moses to Joshua and he prepares to lead the Israelites into the Promised Land, God tells Joshua in no uncertain terms that the Israelites are about to conquer Canaan. Time and again God imparts courage to him through Moses, "Be strong and courageous. Do not be frightened, and do not be dismayed, for the Lord your God is with you wherever you go" (Josh. 1:9). It is easy to read that verse and want to claim it for ourselves, and we should. But first we need to see what it meant for Joshua in his context. God is not just giving him a leadership pep talk; he is asking Joshua to participate—and to recruit all of Israel to do the same. God is asking them to conquer, possess, and take over the entire Promised Land. He is asking them to fight for that which God had already promised.

Like Joshua, we have been called to conquer and possess something that is already promised to us. But unlike Joshua, who was called to actually slay his enemies, the fight step is not about crusades or even culture wars. Rather it is about fighting against evil and fighting for good in the world. We are to fight *for* all that is beautiful and good and true and *against* all that is ugly and bad and false—not just outside of us, but inside our own hearts as well. Just as we saw with the Believe step, there is far more going on in the supernatural realm than we are aware of in our day-to-day living. When we fight against evil in this earthly realm, we are participating in the grand battle of good versus evil that is going on in the heavenly realm. And this fight will continue until God's ultimate vanquishing of Satan and wickedness when Jesus returns.

Joshua knew enough of the history of God's covenant with Israel to know the conquering of the Promised Land would come to pass. He knew that if his promise-keeping God said it, he was going to see victory—no ifs, ands, or buts. Remember, Joshua was one of only two spies who believed God would come through even though the cities were fortified (Num. 14:6–9). However—don't miss it—Joshua and Israel still had to engage in battle. Human responsibility still mattered. The fight would still be costly even though the victory was promised in the Lord. While the motivation and the confidence to engage in the battle was all because of the promises of grace, they still had to *actually fight*. If we look back to Numbers 21 once again, we remember that as a result of being healed of the snake venom through repentance and faith, there was indeed now a life to live (Num. 21:8–9).

We are to fight for all that is beautiful and good and true and against all that is ugly and bad and false—not just outside of us, but inside our own hearts as well.

At the end of Joshua we read that every single promise God had given had come to pass; not one of them failed (Josh. 21:45; 23:14). In the final analysis after the Promised Land has been conquered, Joshua credits their victory to one thing alone: God's gracious promise. And yet that does not minimize the fact that Israel had to fight.

The historical appropriating of the Promised Land is a great metaphor for how we appropriate the promises of the gospel (Eph. 1:11; Heb. 3:7–4:11). Christ guaranteed the blessings of grace for us as our spiritual inheritance, just like God guaranteed the Promised Land. But just as the Israelites still had to take hold of the land, you and I are called to fight the good fight of faith in order to more fully experience the blessings that Christ has already purchased for us (1 Tim. 6:12).

There is some mystery here.

Christ fully purchased our entire salvation through his obedient life and substitutionary death. Yet to enter into the full experience of that salvation, we must fight to possess what Christ has already purchased. However, we are not in any way saved by our own efforts. Confused? Read on.

But Why Call It the *Fight* Step?

Hal Moore was a Lt. Colonel in the U.S. Army in the Vietnam War. In November of 1965 he led his 450 troops into one of the bloodiest battles in the history of American warfare, the battle of La Drang. Not long after Moore and his men were dropped on the battlefield, a recon mission revealed the Army had made a grave mistake by attacking an enemy made up of more than 2,000 troops—far too strong for the Americans. Nonetheless, Moore, who was later chosen as one of the 100 greatest generals in history, led his group to an unlikely victory. A reporter went along with Moore and his troops to take pictures to give Americans back home a taste of the war. After all, this was supposed to be a walk in the park. The reporter snapped pictures as the enemy descended—capturing heavy casualties, gunfire all around, and American soldiers dropping like flies. At one point, the fight was so intense that the camera was shot from his hands; he curled up in the fetal position with his hands over his head. It was at this point that Sergeant Major Plumley, standing in midst of the bullets whizzing by, said to him, "You can't take no pictures lying down there, sonny." Then the sergeant grabbed a gun and threw it into the reporter's hands. The reporter responded, "I'm a non-combatant, sir." To which the sergeant replied, "Ain't no such thing today, boy."

Nothing could be truer of the Christian life. We do not always know what we signed up for, but when Christ calls us to himself by his grace and grants us a new heart, we are enlisted in the army of God. In 2 Timothy 2:1–4 Paul urges Christians to conduct themselves like good soldiers of Christ Jesus. Good soldiers seek to please their commanding officer because good soldiers trust their commanding officer's knowledge, experience, intel, wisdom, and oversight. Brother or sister, we are soldiers.

Make no mistake: we do not fight for acceptance from our Commanding Officer; we fight *from* acceptance. But fight we must, because there are no non-combatants. There is an enemy, Satan, who is bent on our destruction and the destruction of everyone and everything we hold dear. He is sinister and he is superhuman. He has an army of warriors, and he is relentless. He will not stop until he takes his best shot at everything that is beautiful and good and true in God's world. What wonder of grace that we have a good and mighty warrior King. It is well worth it to fight on his side because the end is already decided: he will win the battle.

So why do we call this third step of the Gospel Waltz the Fight step? The term comes from Scripture—from all the places where we are called to engage in battle. In Galatians 5:17, Paul says the desires of the flesh are against those of the Spirit, and the Spirit wars against the desires of the flesh. These two forces are opposed to each other. They are fighting each other; they are at war with each other. Peter says much the same thing in 1 Peter 2:11, where he writes that the passions of the flesh wage war against your soul. In 2 Corinthians 10:3–4, Paul says we do wage war, but not according to human means. In 2 Timothy 2, where Paul is writing about being strong in grace, he reminds us that we are soldiers of Jesus Christ. Part of following Jesus is knowing that there is a war for our souls, that we are soldiers, and that we are called to fight.

Christ's own battle on the cross against sin, death, and Satan did not merely purchase our conversion once and for all; it also guaranteed our ongoing growth in holiness. 1 Corinthians 1:30 reminds us that Jesus is our sanctification. One of the gifts that we are given when we put our trust in Christ is the guarantee that day by day, week by week, month by month, year by year, we will grow in holiness. It is guaranteed because it does not depend on us. It is a gift of God that is given to us when we receive Christ by faith. In other words, the emphasis is not on *how much* work and effort we put in, but rather on *whose strength* that work depends. As Christians, we now have a new pool of life within us. We have been given new hearts, and this is the reality of regeneration (Ezek. 36:24–27; Titus 3:5). In Matthew 12, Jesus says a good tree cannot bear bad fruit, and a bad tree cannot bear good fruit. Because this is true, when we received Christ we received the promise that God *will* bear good fruit in our hearts. A fruitful Christian life is part of the Promised Land that Christ purchased for us on the cross.

When we say that our ongoing growth in holiness has been purchased by Christ and that the emphasis is on whose strength our effort depends, we do not mean that there is no place for our effort in the Christian life. Peter tells us that we are to *make every effort* to add to what is primary, our faith, a host of virtues (2 Peter 1:5–7). This is part of the Fight step of the waltz. We are to work out our salvation because we are confident that God is working in us (Phil. 2:12–13). We are to strive for the holiness without which no one will see the Lord (Heb. 12:14). Titus 2:11–12 shows us that grace trains us to renounce ungodliness and worldly passions and to live self-controlled, upright, and godly lives.

Paul picks up this theme in Galatians 5:23 when he contrasts the work of the flesh with the fruit of the Spirit saying, "Against such things there is no law," meaning no law can produce this fruit because you cannot behave yourself into a changed heart. Lasting fruit is never *primarily* the result of strenuous effort on the part of the believer—that is merely secular behaviorism. Anyone with self-discipline can behave themselves into new disciplines, or even new behaviors. But no one, no matter how great their self-discipline, can transform their inner heart or innermost person. The only way a heart can be changed and bear the fruit of the Spirit is by receiving it, appropriating it, and believing that it is part of the blessing of what we received when we trusted in Christ. This is why Francis Schaeffer described the Christian life as *active passivism*. The paradigm of the gospel is this: constantly exercising an active faith in the already-finished promise of God.

I am a die-hard Penn State fan; I grew up in State College, Pennsylvania. I am such a huge fan that I record all of Penn State's football games, whether or not I get to watch live. Curiously, I enjoy the game even more when I know they win before I get to watch it. I have found that when I know they win, the battlefield mistakes do not discourage me or deter me the way they would when I am watching a live game. Christian: we have this same assurance. When it comes to the battle we face on a daily basis, we know that Christ has already won the victory. That means we can fight the good fight with confidence, assurance, peace, and joy even when the battle is intense.

The only way a heart can be changed and bear the fruit of the Spirit is by receiving it, appropriating it, and believing that it is part of the blessing of what we received when we trusted in Christ.

The Scriptures are filled with imperatives, commands, and prohibitions. This is the kind of life we are now free to live, and grace will give us the desire to follow this God-given path. The commands are an invitation to our highest delight, and the prohibitions are a warning against our worst nightmare. We know this because God loves us and only has our best interests at heart. What are some of these commands?

Speak the truth. Ex. 20:16; Eph. 4:15, 25

Be others-centered. Phil. 2:3–4

Do not let the sun go down on your anger. Ps. 37:8;

Eph. 4:26; James 1:20

Do not steal. Ex. 20:15; Mark 10:19

Share every good thing. Prov. 22:9; Isa. 58:7; Luke 3:11; Eph. 4:28

Work hard. Acts 20:35

Watch your tongue. Ps. 39:1; James 1:26; James 3:5–8; 1 Pet. 3:10

Share your faith. Matt. 28:18–20; 1 Pet. 3:15–16; 2 Tim. 1:7–8

Know the Scriptures. 2 Tim. 2:15; Col. 3:16

Be filled with the Spirit. Eph. 5:18; Gal. 5:16

Gather regularly for worship. Ex. 20:8–11; Deut. 31:12–13; Heb. 10:25

Renew your minds. Rom. 12:2; Eph. 4:23

If married, love and respect your spouse. Eph. 5:22–31; 1 Pet. 3:1–7

If parents, raise your children in the fear and admonition of the Lord. Eph. 6:4; Deut. 6:6–7; Col. 3:21

Remember the poor. Lev. 19:10; Ps. 41:1; Gal. 2:10

Bear one another's burdens. Gal. 6:2; Rom. 15:1

Use your Spirit-given gifts in serving the church and the world. 1 Pet. 4:10; Rom. 12:6

Do your work unto the Lord. Col. 3:23

Clearly the commands of Scripture are abundant. However, many churches have the order all out of whack. We cannot jump immediately to the gospel imperatives; we must progress in order—getting both Repent and Believe square before we even begin to talk about Fight. If we fail to do so, we will find ourselves living on a ladder where "Fight" is the pinnacle of the Christian life, rather than moving through the circular dance of the Gospel Waltz. However, if we fail to know and emphasize the commands of God, we can get all out of whack in the other direction.

Climb On Out of the Hot Tub

While some may want to skip over the Repent and Believe steps straight to behaviors, others of us may experience a pull to never leave those steps, being lured into a spiritual passivism. I like to refer to this extreme as "Life in the Christian Hot Tub." If you have ever hopped into a Jacuzzi after a brutal workout or stressful day, you know the soothing warmth of the bubbling water on your aching or tense muscles. It is so relaxing that you just want to sit and soak . . . forever.

Similarly, when people have come out of a stressful, performance-based paradigm of Christian living and hear about grace for the Christian life, the soothing waters of the gospel feel so restorative that they just want to sit and soak, soak, soak. But, just like the warning sticker on the side of any hot tub about the dangers of staying in too long, we also need to be warned about sitting and soaking in the message of grace as unconditional love without getting out and getting on with the obedience of faith. We must allow the soothing waters of grace to lead us out of the hot tub and into transformational repentance and belief, which can then lead us to engage with the Fight step in a healthy way.

A friend and fellow pastor named Phil came out of a performance-based ministry during his college years. As the living waters of grace began to massage away his obsessive behaviorism, he realized that his devotional life needed a tune-up—but not the kind you might think. Phil realized that what had been given to him as a *means of* grace (the invitation to devotional life), he had turned into a *work-in-exchange-for* grace. In the depths of his thought life, Phil had begun to believe that God would bless him in the circumstances of his life and prevent hardships only if he was faithful in his quiet time. All bets were off for experiencing any favor throughout the day should he fail in his devotional pursuits. He had to work for it.

The Holy Spirit then used a fresh gospel emphasis Phil had begun to marinate in to call him to a unique response. For a brief season, Phil stopped engaging in devotional time in order to force himself to rest in the finished work of Christ and God's kind disposition toward him as a son, entirely apart from his performance. He completely stopped working for it, but he also completely . . . *stopped.*

After a time of backing away from pursuing God in his Word, my friend shared with me what had been going on. While I do not recommend engaging in such a "sabbatical," I rejoiced with him at the life-changing revelation of the Father toward him and the freedom he was experiencing. Having been enslaved to a similar try-harder mentality myself many times while trying to craft a perfect sermon, I was able to ask my friend a couple questions that I ask of myself when I find I am engaging with the folly of a performance-oriented connection. Phil was transparent with me about the specifics of how long his Scripture-sabbatical had been, what other pursuits he had filled this time with, and how he had seen both positive and negative impact from this backing away. Graciously, our discussion did a work in my own heart as it reminded me of my own freedom in the gospel. But then—as his friend and fellow traveler—I asked a question I have had to ask of myself many times: as you sit and soak in grace, are you pruning up? We were able to connect over the importance of moving along and not staying too long in the Hot Tub.

By grace, when my friend re-engaged with his devotional life again, he found entirely new motives. Phil found he had been given a new appreciation for God's work through his Word that had absolutely nothing to do with his own worthiness in pursuing it. Phil was no longer spending time with Jesus in order to get favor but out of love for the God who already promised to favor him because of the work of Christ.

Two Kinds of Righteousness

The hot tub leads us to consider two kinds of righteousness in the gospel: passive and active righteousness.

Passive righteousness is the righteousness that we did not lift a finger to achieve but can only receive. Christ achieved and attained it for us—that is why theologians call it passive. As children of God united to Christ, we have a righteousness that comes from Christ and is through faith. It does not increase over time but is fully imputed to us at conversion. Because passive righteousness involves no works of our own, it is akin to the warm waters of the message of grace as unconditional love. And it is *so passive*, that if we try to add any righteousness of our own to it, we ruin it and immediately shift into a performance paradigm.

So often, I can slip into this paradigm at a moment's notice, looking for a momentary sense of acceptance by trying to add to my own righteousness through some work. I am embarrassed to say how many times I have tried to make myself look a little better than I actually am when running into a church member who has been disconnected from our church fellowship. "I was just going to call you!"—I am often tempted to say, when the truth is, sure, I had thought of calling them, but had failed to follow through. Many times, it is as if Jesus and the gospel mean nothing to my soul as I struggle to admit my wrong and simply say, "I'm so sorry I haven't called." Just as God told the Israelites over and over and over to remember him, so we return in our moments of forgetting to the truth of the gospel so that we can be settled in our passive righteousness before we begin to pursue acts of righteousness.

Whereas passive righteousness is imputed to us, active righteousness is a righteousness imparted to us that increases over time as we engage in repentance and faith and step out in new obedience.

Once the passive righteousness is settled, we come to the Fight step of the Waltz. Because, as those who are righteous in Christ, we *are* called to pursue acts of righteousness. There is a righteousness that we are responsible to pursue, known as active righteousness. Whereas passive righteousness is *imputed* to us, active righteousness is a righteousness *imparted* to us that increases over time as we engage in repentance and faith and step out in new obedience. Active righteousness involves us energetically pursuing godly virtues and rigorously fighting our own sin.

As we sit and soak in our passive righteousness, the Holy Spirit, by grace, also leads us to get out of the hot tub; he moves us into active righteousness. It is a righteousness that we *can* pursue because as we gaze upon Christ, supernatural, transforming, resurrection power flows into our lives in abundance. As we pursue active righteousness and embrace Christ's power, we find we can truly live—just like in Numbers 21, "whoever looks shall live." This is not just continuing as before or just existing and not dying; it is true, Christ-empowered abundant living.

Once God has said, "Your righteousness has been accomplished," he then says "Now do it." That is very different from what many of us hear, which is "Just do it." "Just do it" has no power because it is out of our own efforts, which are certain to fail. Even if we think it works, it is out of self-effort and not out of faith, which undoes the entire basis of our relationship with Christ. "*Now* do it" is a totally different story, because it has all the power of the Trinity behind it, and it brings forth life and godliness: *In light of acknowledging your sin, in light of your putting hope in Christ and the power of the Holy Spirit,* now do it. *Set your will to follow biblical principles in a dependent striving.*

But what does this tension look like in actuality as we move about our day? Well, I can tell you what it looks like for me in an area of great struggle: anxiety.

My daughter, Hannah, has given me many opportunities over our dear years together to be stretched in both passive and active righteousness. Hannah is a go-getter with big ideas and big dreams. When she was younger she rode horses and participated in equestrian sports, including show jumping. Of course this drove me nuts with anxiety because I am more of a let's-not-fall-off-a-horse kind of guy. In college, Hannah became deeply involved in the ministry of the International Justice Mission, even helping to start the chapter at her college, Auburn University. Her work led her into further adventure in central Africa—and led me into further anxiety as she spent two years helping women and children in dangerous circumstances.

Let's just say from showjumping to anti-trafficking work in Africa to many instances in between, God has used Hannah's fearlessness to expose my control issues. It has been nothing short of a battle for me to remember that God was just as much in command of the circumstances of Hannah in Africa as he was over Michael at Belmont University. That he had Josh at his first job and my wife and I in the basement as the tornado bore down on our home. That he has our church and our home and now, my precious grandchildren. He is orchestrating a plan far grander and greater than I could concoct—all for his glory and our good. I have to fight to *actively* believe that he has got us and I do not need to fret or attempt to orchestrate circumstances. I can simply *passively* receive the promises of that which I could never truly orchestrate—God's ultimate protection of myself and those I love. I receive the gift of what I cannot earn—the ability to trust God with my family—and I can actively pursue that which God enables me to do as I take up my sword and fight against control. It is a fight I need to engage in over and over again.

How can we practically do this? First, we can memorize Scripture. Dwelling on verses about God's peace and sovereignty was specifically helpful to me in fighting my anxiety. Second, we can pray. Third, we can ask others to pray for us, especially the elders of our church (James 5:13–18). Fourth, we may even engage in some fasting in order to increase our desperation for Jesus to increase the Spirit's fruit of peace in our life. Fifth, we might consider taking the step of seeking a Christian counselor to help us to pursue active righteousness (this can be especially helpful in dealing with anxiety). These are just some of the ways we can engage in the Fight step.

As we Repent, Believe, and Fight, we begin to experience grace not merely as unconditional love, but also as transforming power to live godly lives. And as we waltz through the disciplines of grace (read and memorize Scripture, pray, engage in public and private worship, give generously, practice fasting, simplicity, and silence, etc.), godliness grows within us. Truly, it is only after we are freed from our performance paradigm that we are able to engage in the disciplines in a right fashion. The disciplines are not something strong Christians do to prove to God that they are worthy of his blessing. The disciplines of grace are what weak and humble Christians must engage in as means of feeding on and drinking of Christ and his benefits more deeply.

How We Fight: Christian Passivism and Christian Activism

There is a curious trend in the modern church in regard to righteousness—one that I am going to split in half since most people view it from one of two vantage points. For the sake of the discussion, we will call these outlooks Christian Passivism ("let go and let God"), and Christian Activism ("I can do it, God can help").

Our Brokenness Is Not Our Whole Story

Some of us naturally lean toward Christian Passivism and are quick to "let go and let God," just like we saw in one of the Bunny Hop false dances. Like the Corinthians or those Paul refers to in Romans 6:1, this view has a libertine or a passive perception of the Christian life. Often, these folks have a version of the supernatural life that sees people as lifeless sticks that just need to catch the current so the flow of the Holy Spirit will move us along. Or people mistakenly think that the Holy Spirit will just "zap" them with power and they will automatically live a godly life. Or, it could be that they feel God is just okay with their brokenness and they do not need to worry about it so much. Some may not even be convinced that the Christian life is to involve such effort—it is just too hard to fight back against sin. Others may leave no room for fighting besetting sins and even take the view that, "This is just the way I am. I'm growing in other areas like patience and contentment, but when it comes to anger, it's just going to always be with me and I've accepted that." No matter the slant, what Christian Passivists tend to be well aware of is their brokenness.

It seems it has become trendy to speak of our brokenness in the modern church. It is cool to be transparent and vulnerable, even one-upping each other about just how awful we are. Now, in proper context and measure, vulnerability can be one of the most beautiful gifts of the modern church. In James 5:16 we see we are to confess our sins to one another so that we may experience healing. In a gospel-driven church that emphasizes grace, there should be authenticity and transparency. There should be a sense in which I do not need to impress you, you do not need to impress me, and we can be honest about the battle we face with the flesh. But brokenness in the modern church can be elevated to an unhealthy level when it becomes the whole story.

Our brokenness is not the end of the story. Our brokenness is not even what the gospel is all about. Sure, brokenness is part of our story, but it is not our whole story. The gospel is about Jesus making all things new. Our need is simply what necessitates it, not what defines it. We are a people who are on our way to becoming, in this life, exactly whom God desires us to be. As believers in Jesus, indwelt by the personal presence of the Holy Spirit, we can give testimony to the power of grace in us to enable us to say no to sin. This is far more powerful than vulnerability for vulnerability's sake.

I will never forget the night of our wedding as Laurie and I prepared to drive away from the church to head out for our honeymoon. As we ran through the rain of rice from friends and extended family, we suddenly heard frantic screaming coming from the small children around us: they were covered by red ants.

If you have ever seen a child or a toddler bitten by scores of fire ants, you know that you must react—and fast. You must tear off those children's shoes and socks and clothing because nothing is more important than freeing them from the danger of the ants.

When Paul says we are to put off the old self in Ephesians 4:22 and Colossians 3:9, what he is describing is a violent tearing, a renouncing, and a throwing of the old self far from you—likely in dramatic fashion. Just like the clothing items covered by those ants, we must remove sin intentionally and quickly with our minds fixed on nothing else.

This charge leaves little room for wallowing in brokenness. Yes, we are needy, but yes—even more so—glory to God who met that need and now invites us to participate in our own sanctification by stripping off the old man.[22] Paul's words leave little room for the "let go and let God" of Christian Passivism. Glory to God who has a plan to redeem, restore, and transform us. That must be just as much a part of the story of a gospel-driven church as the stories of brokenness.

When All You Hear Is "Do, Do, Do"

Sadly, when some of us get to the Fight step of the Waltz, we break out in a cold sweat. For some of us, it feels like we are being called right back into a performance paradigm all over again—as Christian Activism can turn into a behavioral view of Christianity that many of us are comfortable with and some of us have become burned-out on. Perhaps it is because we have been heavy-footed fighters our whole lives, or because all throughout our Christian experience we have been part of churches that have emphasized trying harder and doing more.

If your palms are starting to sweat, I completely understand. I came out of a performance mentality where trying harder was my Bunny Hop. When God began to call me into the gospel-centered life and I realized that there really is a life to live (Titus 2:11–3:8), my own palms began to sweat. It felt like an invitation to performance all over again. I struggled to

---

[22] Romans 8:13: "If by the Spirit you put to death the deeds of the body, you will live." Our sanctification is by the Spirit, but we do it, we act on it!

think of obedience and discipline apart from merit and maintaining or earning the Father's delight. But as I continued to flounder and splash about in the waters of grace, feeling like I still might drown, God kindly revealed to me that I was no longer on Planet Performance. I was on a different planet—actually, I was in a different universe. God kept mercifully reminding me that I was no longer doing/fighting *for* acceptance, but that he was inviting me to continue doing/fighting *from* acceptance. I was using my renewed will flowing from my regenerate heart and my new confidence in the Spirit to engage life. And yes, it did feel to me, a heavy footed fighter, like, "Oh no, here we go again." And that is where we need to talk each other off the ledge. The gospel says our position with the Father is secure. So now, depending upon the Spirit, we can fight *from* a position of acceptance and not *for* it.

For those of us who are coming out of a paradigm of trying harder, the Fight step may feel like legalism, like being called back to a paradigm of earning through effort. If we define legalism as thinking that our obedience gains us points with God, then the call to obedience in the gospel is never legalism, it is just a call to fight the good fight of faith. Again, this is why the use of the word "Fight" as the third step of the Gospel Waltz is so revolutionary. We obey a call to pursue active righteousness as those who have already been declared passively righteous. Though it may feel like it, there really is no tension between the call to obedience and the grace of God, and part of our fighting the good fight of faith may be to remind ourselves of this very thing!

Grace and obedience are not a dichotomy. Let's consider Titus 2:11–14 again. The passage gives us a beautiful model of the progression of salvation by grace toward obedient actions of holiness from a position of love and gratitude. Titus 2:11 and 14 say, "For the grace of God [Christ himself] has appeared . . . to redeem us from all lawlessness and to purify for himself a people for his own possession who are zealous for good works." Grace is actually what leads to good works. Grace transforms us because it is not simply a concept, but rather a sphere of power we stand in (Rom. 5:2).

Paul says that we died to that old, condemning relationship we had to the law (Rom. 7:1–4). All the law did was expose failure and show us how much we are condemned under God's wrath because of our sin. Paul says that as Christians we have a new relationship to the law. There is no power in the law to change us, but our relationship to it has been changed. As the law reveals the holiness of God and his nature, it also reveals our sin and shows us how desperately we need the work of Christ to continue in our lives.

The secret word is integration. It is the theme that keeps us from heavy-footedness, and it is the primary tenet of the Gospel Waltz. God longs to show us how to waltz with him in an even-footed, flowing manner.

What Are We Fighting Against? The Roles of the Flesh and the World.

There has been a lot of talk about battle and warfare in this Fight chapter of the Gospel Waltz. But what or who exactly are we fighting against? James 4:1–10 defines our enemies as the flesh, the world, and the devil.[23] We tend to be quite familiar with the ways that the world

---

[23] Ligonier Ministries, https://www.ligonier.org/learn/devotionals/world-flesh-and-devil.

tempts us to sin (James 4:4), but less familiar with the ways our flesh participates. First we will focus on the flesh, and then we will address Satan's role.

The flesh sums up the part of the human nature that is still in rebellion to God. In verse 1 James says the problem we have as Christians is that our passions are at work within us. Even as a believer, there are surprisingly powerful evil inclinations that reside within each of us. Those passions and impulses will never disappear in this life. It will not be until we are made completely new, when Christ returns or calls us home, that those will disappear. The flesh can't be reformed, but it can be resisted. In Scripture the flesh is presented not as mere brokenness, but as an indwelling power, a residual resistance to God that he mysteriously leaves with the believer after conversion. The flesh does not decrease throughout the Christian's life, but our capacity to say no to it can increase as we waltz. This is why theologians remind us that though it is true that we are called saints in Christ (positionally), we are still also called sinners (in our daily condition). Martin Luther used the Latin phrase, *simul justus et peccator. Simul* means simultaneously. *Justis* means just or righteous. *Et* means and. *Peccator* means sinner. So, as R.C. Sproul writes, "with this formula, Luther was saying, in our justification we are at one and the same time righteous or just, and sinners."[24] There are redeemed sinners and there are unredeemed sinners. There are repentant sinners

The flesh can't be reformed, but it can be resisted.

[24] R.C. Sproul, 10/17/19, https://www.ligonier.org/posts/simul-justus-et-peccator.

and there are unrepentant sinners. We will be sinners until the day we die. Even if we cannot stop the impulses, Scripture tells us that we possess a new heart and are indwelt with a new power to say no to them (1 John 5:4). We must fight against the power of the flesh that remains within us. Romans 8:13 shows us we are not lifeless sticks floating effortlessly down the current of life, but rather we can and must "by the Spirit, put to death the deeds of the body." It is important that we understand that Paul says by the Spirit you and I are to put to death the deeds of the flesh. It is by the Spirit—that is, the Spirit empowers us to do it—but we must also be actively involved in the process. There is a mystery of divine power and human choice and effort. Galatians 5:16 says, "Walk by the Spirit, and you will not carry out the desires of the flesh," and Ephesians 4:22 says, "Put off the old self."

Non-Christians are only flesh. They solely operate out of fleshly impulse. But Christians are genuinely new creations that, though we still possess sinful desires that we will not be rid of until Christ returns or calls us home, by God's providence we are no longer ruled by those desires. Though sin still dwells within us and seeks to influence our thoughts, feelings, longings, and choices, the flesh in a Christian can be overcome by the Spirit as we walk in the power of the Spirit . . . as we Waltz.

In this lifelong battle we must constantly be reminded that the flesh is not merely the lure of "bad" sins. The flesh is actually a two-sided coin of both religiosity and irreligiosity. Put another way, the flesh pulls us toward the ditch of legalism and self-righteousness in one moment and toward the ditch of libertinism and self-indulgence the next. I have discovered in my years as a Christian that the longer someone has been a believer, the bigger temptation is often toward legalism, not license, though clearly both remain dangers through our entire lives. We fight against the flesh.

Who Are We Fighting Against?

If you are a Christian, you live with a bullseye on your back. Satan hates you unlike anyone on this planet has ever hated you. He hates your walk with Christ, he hates your marriage, he hates your career, he hates your children, he hates your contentment in your singleness, he hates your faithfulness in your infertility, and he hates the very image of you. Satan hates everything about you, and you are a marked man, woman, or child.

In our fight against Satan, sometimes it can feel hard to remember or even believe that because of the work of Christ, God has given us the upper hand against the enemy (Col. 2:15, 1 John 4:4). Jesus speaks of Satan's realm, hell, and its already/not yet destruction in Matthew 16 when he says with certain confidence, "I will build my church, and the gates of hell shall not prevail against it." Notice that we, the Church, are on the offensive in the battle. Revelation 20:7–10 speaks of the sure destruction of Satan and his ultimate demise. Unlike God, the devil has an end point. Unlike our King, his power has limits. We worship the One who is everything Satan is not—just, true, faithful, loving, merciful, and kind. We worship the God who helps us in our fight against the kingdom of darkness. "Resist the devil and he will flee from you," James 4:7 promises, and God is faithful to teach us exactly how to do so. We must become people, churches, friends, and homes that pray and appropriate the promises of God in Scripture.

What Are We Fighting For?

Though it is vastly important to know what we are fighting against, it is even more important to know what we are fighting for. Our definition of grace needs to be holistic, one that makes motion in a positive direction, not just in a defensive one.

Christians should be known more for what we are *for* rather than what we are *against*. The Christian life is more than just saying "no" to common sins like the "nasty nines and the dirty dozens and filthy fives," especially when the yes's of God's goodness are far more appealing and lasting. We are *for* the beauty of righteousness. We are *for* the attractiveness of godliness. We are *for* the pursuit of holiness in all realms of life so as to show love back to God. Titus 2 says that not only does grace train us to say "no" to ungodliness and worldly passions, but grace also trains us to live upright, self-controlled, godly lives.

But when it all comes down to it, *what are we saying yes to*? How can we set our minds and our wills toward godliness without just making a tidy list that addresses outward behavior rather than inward change? When we seek to abide in Christ, we seek far more than just behaviors. Behaviors will not draw the heart toward intimacy with the living God; they will not change your heart. In truth, they exist in every religion in the world and in every self-help book. No, we seek principles that can guide rather than boxes that might be checked. As C. S. Lewis says in *Mere Christianity*:

> [To have faith in Christ] means, of course, trying to do all that he says. There would be no sense in saying you trusted a person if you would not take his advice. Thus if you have really handed yourself over to him, it must follow that you are trying to obey him. But trying in a new way, a less worried way. Not doing these things in order to be saved, but because he has begun to save you already. Not hoping to get to heaven as a reward for your actions, but inevitably wanting to act in a certain way because a first faint gleam of heaven is already inside you.[25]

Commit to Saying "Yes" to Submission

Instead of submitting to our own sinful desires, as Christians we submit to the lordship of Christ and his perspective on the commands of Scripture (James 4:7). We often hear the word "surrender" and think it is a giving up and giving in to an opponent that has overcome us. But when God asks us to submit, the differences could not be more vital: the One asking us to surrender is not our opponent at all but our Champion. He is all-wise and all-knowing and is asking us to trust him with his course of action, to follow him onto the battlefield in which he has already been named the victor. Our submission comes in trusting and following the One who is trustworthy rather than leaning on our own understanding of both ourselves and our circumstances. We are submitting to the will of a loving Father that is good and acceptable and perfect (Rom. 12:2). When we submit to God's commands we are submitting to our highest pleasure, and

[25] C. S. Lewis, *Mere Christianity* (San Francisco: Harper, 2001), 147.

when we submit to God's prohibitions we are avoiding our worst nightmares.

Counter to what the world says, when we fight to say yes to submission to God's will, we are actually fighting for our freedom. The freedom we have been called to in Christ is both a freedom *from* and a freedom *for*. It is freedom from condemnation, shame, self-righteousness, and self-indulgence, and it is also freedom for righteousness, obedience, love, and an integrated heart.

Commit to saying "Yes" to Intimacy

Drawing near to God (James 4:8) is something we do primarily by faith—by believing the gospel promises. But we also draw near to God by the means of grace (e.g., worship, prayer, reading Scripture, spending time devotionally with God, or even having a gospel conversation with a friend). These means of grace are activities we participate in that can certainly make us feel near to God, but they by no means make God draw more near to us. We do not "earn points" for them, but they do cultivate a condition of the heart that longs to be near him—that longs for more grace and therefore more means of grace. Our union with Christ is unchanging, but our experience of fellowship and intimacy with him can dwindle when we are not drawing near. The Fight step of The Waltz includes all the means of grace, or spiritual disciplines, that most of us have been taught throughout our entire Christian lives.

But it is not just intimacy with God we pursue as we seek to abide; it is also intimacy with one another through God's gift of transforming community: the church. When we are engaged in healthy and growing Christian relationships in corporate worship, small groups, service opportunities, and one-on-one discipleship, we will experience transformation through the Spirit's activity in the hearts and lives of our brothers and sisters in Christ. As we waltz with Jesus in the ballroom of the church, we look around and realize we are not alone. We are never alone because we are always waltzing alongside other couples—our believing friends and family who are likewise engaged in their own dance with Christ. We need the voices of our gospel community reminding us of the truth at our lowest moments, encouraging us to stay in the fight, asking us the hard questions, and lifting us up in prayer.

Commit to saying "Yes" to Purity

As Dallas Willard reminds us, "Grace is not opposed to effort. It is opposed to earning. Effort is action. Earning is attitude. You have never seen people more active than those who have been set on fire by the grace of God."[26] As we seek to honor Christ with our lives, we are to make daily, moment-by-moment decisions to pursue godliness, holiness, and righteousness. This purity is actually far more than what most evangelicals think of when they think of purity. We have sanitized holiness—especially where I live, in the Bible Belt—when God's demands for holiness are far greater than we could ever imagine.

Purity is fighting to keep our eyes fixed on Christ. It is asking God to give us the energy to dependently pursue holiness in the particulars (Rom. 6:19). It is moving toward and growing in the means of grace, relationships, missional living, Christ-centered ethics, and moderation in all things. It is loving the poor,

[26] Dallas Willard, *Renewing the Christian Mind* (HarperCollins, 2016), 17.

helping the oppressed, fighting for the defenseless. If you are feeling any shame or overwhelm at the thought of this degree of the pursuit of purity—that is great news! As I experience the same, I want to fight to view that overwhelm simply as an invitation to waltz yet again. Fighting for purity is such an overwhelming task that if we are actively fighting to keep our eyes fixed on Christ, we will immediately realize just how short we fall. We will be overcome by his majesty and underwhelmed by our efforts, and we will be kicked right back into the repent step of the Gospel Waltz, only to begin the 1, 2, 3 all over again, in mercy and grace and his never-ending pursuit of us.

Because God is at work in us, we are able to "work out our salvation with fear and trembling" (Phil. 2:12–13). Unfortunately, this popular translation of "fear and trembling" can make us feel the knee-jerk reaction, "Oh no! I'm going to fail this thing." If you are a performance-junkie like me, a better translation might be, "Work out your salvation with wonder and awe, because the God of the universe is at work in you, enabling you to will and to work according to his good pleasure." The only reason we are able to work is because God is in fact at work within us. This is why Paul says in Galatians 5:25, "If we live by the Spirit, let us also keep in step with the Spirit." Our old natures have been crucified. We are able, because we have new hearts in the Holy Spirit, to say yes to righteousness and obedience and holiness.

Whose Strength Are We Fighting With?

Most people think that a worm crawling down the branch of a tree begins to bore its way into the apple, and that is how the worm gets access. In actuality, when there is an apple blossom on an apple tree, there is a small insect that flies into the apple blossom. Then the apple actually grows around the insect, the insect turns into a worm, and the worm eats its way out from the inside. I hope we can see this negative illustration in a positive light, because it perfectly describes the work of the Holy Spirit. It is an inside job.

When we trusted in Christ we were given the Spirit of God, and the Spirit of God is in fact working in our lives. But we still have a big problem. We are sometimes so filled with doubt that we are constantly checking—*Is he at work? Is it happening? Is it growing? Am I sure? Where is it?*—instead of simply resting in what God promised and trusting that he is faithful to accomplish it. The Christian life is a counter-intuitive life of faith.

Now, I hope your experience is not the same, but I find golf so frustrating. Half the time I don't know whether to break my clubs or throw them into one of those tiny golf course ponds. In golf, it would seem that the harder you hit the ball, the farther it will go. But, as it turns out—at least for all of us non-professionals—it does not matter how hard you swing. You are simply supposed to swing, and the ball is supposed to get in the way of the swing. If you try intently to hit the ball hard, you never will. Similarly, in the Christian life, the harder you try sometimes, the worse your Christian life goes. The only way the Christian life is going to be formed in us is as we look to God and trust him by his Spirit to form it into our lives. Therefore we can fight from a place of deep soul rest.

Friends of Jesus, by the regenerating power of God we have new hearts (Ezek. 36:26; Titus 3:5), we are indwelt by the Holy Spirit, and because of his supernatural changes in our lives, we are actually able to read the Word of God, understand the commands and the prohibitions, and follow them. We are not helpless. We are not victims. The wonder of the gospel is that although on the one hand we are incredibly broken and fallen and we need to live in daily repentance, it is also true that we are incredibly glorious. We have been recreated in Christ with new hearts, new abilities, new natures, new desires, and a new core of our very being, one whose highest honor is to love God and to love others with all of our heart, soul, mind, and strength.

Until the day we are home with Jesus, we too must commit to fighting for our own hearts as well as for the hearts of those we love and even the hearts of those we've never met. Our confidence in God's purposes sets both ourselves and those around us to the perseverance of obedience from love. After all, it is by the grace, mercy, and love of God that we get to join in on the pushing back of evil until that promised day when it can threaten no more.

Chapter 7 Summary

- Grace is not merely unconditional love; it is also the transforming power to live godly lives.
- God calls and enables us to fight the good fight of faith.
- Though sin still dwells within us and seeks to influence our thoughts, feelings, longings, and choices, the flesh in a Christian can be overcome by the Spirit as we walk in the power of the Spirit.

Reflection Questions

1. Describe a time when you bypassed the gospel indicatives (what is true of us in Christ) and went straight to the gospel imperatives (actions and obedience). What was the fruit of this time?
2. Have you ever found yourself pruning up in a hot tub of grace? What kept you in there too long? What helped you move out of the hot tub and into obedience?
3. Do you naturally lean toward Christian Passivism ("let go and let God") or Christian Activism ("I've got this. God can help.")? What might in integrated approach offer?
4. Is there a specific area where you can sense the Spirit inviting you to fight the good fight of faith? What might that look like?
5. In what ways is the Fight step difficult for you? Does it feel like legalism? Does it feel too easy—like it might be your natural, knee-jerk reaction? Or does it feel like the appropriate response of a trust-filled believer?

8

PRACTICE MAKES PROGRESS (NOT PERFECT!)

Karl Wallenda was one of the longest-participating members of the family high wire act, The Flying Wallendas. He continued walking high wires in gigantic stadiums across the world even after experiencing tragic performance incidents involving members of his troupe and family. Into his 70's, Karl was still walking wires in front of tremendous crowds. He once told his wife, "I feel like a dead man when I'm on the ground. Life is being on the wire." Karl knew the risk; he had counted the cost. He had even personally experienced the heartache of great pain and loss, and still—in spite of it all—he was most fully alive up on that wire.

The Christian life is a lot like life on the wire. The Christian life is living the risk of the gospel on a daily basis. We are living high off the ground of this natural world and operating on a human level, from our perspective, without a net. The gospel-centered life is one of counting the cost of denying self, taking up a cross, following whole-heartedly after Christ, and deeming it worthwhile, adding our voice to that of the apostle Peter's: "Lord, to whom shall we go? You have the words of eternal life" (John 6:68). Following Jesus is agreeing to give ourselves over fully to his transforming power. We are risking it all on the promise that the holiness of God must lead to a life of vulnerability, owning our sin and brokenness, and entering into continual repentance. We are surrendering to the risky proposition that the love of God can only lead to belief that any change we experience comes from outside of ourselves and is supernatural. And we are living on the high wire, giving ourselves over to the idea that the transforming power of God will lead to the motivation and ability to fight. *Repent, Believe, Fight, 1, 2, 3.* In Karl Wallenda's wildest dreams, he never could have imagined waltzing on a wire, and yet that is our calling. We waltz on the wire, and it is the most exciting life anybody could be called to. It is our destiny to trust God to such a degree.

Keep On, Keepin' On

As exciting and renewing as waltzing is, waltzing does not fix us; it is simply how broken Christians in a broken world live broken lives, all the while experiencing substantial life change until Christ returns or calls us home. The Waltz is about being renewed day by day through the ever-present and close embrace of Jesus, our Waltz Partner.

Waltzing is a continuous, lifelong process. It is rinse and repeat. We have been called to a risky trust, day by day, moment by moment: the life of being sanctified by Christ. There is no net, there is no "Plan B." It is believing the gospel or bust.

Waltzing is a paradigm of experiencing progressive sanctification. We are all well aware that we will never arrive at perfection in this life. As we engage with Jesus in the waltz we cannot change the reality that in the literal sense, none of us will find heaven on earth before we die. The Waltz will not fix us or make us "arrive," but it can help us understand our ongoing sanctification. Rather than having an "arrival" mentality, we can adopt an "abiding" mentality, in which we keep on following the progression of sanctification which is walking in the Spirit, abiding in Christ, and being renewed day by day.

Isn't renewal what the Christian life is all about? Because I don't know about you, but I don't just want to be loved, or even to possess some perspective akin to Christian triumphalism. I want to be changed. I want to look more like Jesus every day of my life. And until he firmly and finally deals with my indwelling sin and all the world's evil on the final judgment day, he has seen fit to invite me to *keep going.* He invites me to press in, to abide, to dance with him through all the circumstances of my life. It seems that God cares more about me learning to trust Jesus and boast in the gospel than he does about me being fixed in this life. And until that glorious day when he ends all the sadness and hurt and pain, I have been invited to be with him, to continue to experience at a deeper level every day just what he means when he says, "Behold, I am making all things new" (Rev. 21:5).

Waltzing does not fix us; it is simply how broken Christians in a broken world live broken lives, all the while experiencing substantial life change until Christ returns or calls us home.

As I wait, I want to be patient, faithful, and present. I want to engage with the Spirit in the waltz as the invitation to a lifetime of walking with Jesus. When each and every musical note of the circumstances of our lives is simply a part of the symphony of God wooing us, it gives new perspective to trials, difficult seasons, and even celebratory ones. Consider a piece of symphony music. Think of the different movements and the distinct atmospheres and emotions they conjure up. Some parts are short staccato notes, some are melodious chords, and some are only a few seconds long. Other movements are in minor keys with complicated runs and can last until intermission. But this is just like a Christian's waltz with Jesus. Some parts of the symphony are airy, light, and delightful, and others seem to have unexpected notes, segments, or even dissonance. Some can feel hard to dance to. Just as the members of the orchestra must trust the conductor, we must trust in God to time and tune every single note of our lives. Sometimes I have to be told that the music I am hearing is even a waltz, as the rhythm is indiscernible. Perhaps we feel the same way when we waltz for years or even decades over the same area of life.

As we begin to internalize and practice the Gospel Waltz, it is natural for there to be a season where it feels a little mechanical. Just like learning to shoot a jump shot or bake a new recipe, a new practice can seem forced or uncertain at first. But then you begin to understand each of the components a little more, one by one. And as you understand a component more fully, you see how it fits with the next. Perhaps as you get used to the steps of the Waltz you may now begin to reflect on what it means to be heavy footed. Then it is a bit of a quicker discovery of what step you are in and how to move toward the next one more readily. Over time, you will find you can waltz in a matter of seconds. It does not need to take a half day—you can learn how to waltz in the midst of traffic; you can waltz mid-sentence or mid-conversation.

Accept the Invitation to Dance

Think of a little girl dancing in the kitchen with her daddy. As the father is dancing along, she puts her feet on her dad's shoes and lets him lead her. That is what it is like walking with God. That is what it is like abiding in Christ. And that is what it is like waltzing with Jesus. It is all up to him; we just get to follow. He is the lead.

The beauty of repentance is in being filled with amazement as we realize that the moment we least think we deserve the hope of grace, grace is available to us. Then, as we believe in the hope of grace, when we least deserve to believe it, the power of the Holy Spirit brings about spiritual revolution. And then as we believe God wants to renew us, we are led into the Fight step, where we are called by the Spirit to put to death the deeds of the body and believe in his goodness to change us. We are not sitting around waiting to be changed. Oh no, we are waltzing, inviting change, asking to be held closer and tighter, feeling more of the security of the embrace.

Waltzing in Community

But as we have seen, we never want to pursue this Christian life alone. Waltzing alone is never as fun as waltzing in a ballroom filled with friends. The church is our ballroom, and it is packed with our brothers and sisters in Christ. Sometimes it is helpful for a couple to even pause and back up to observe another particularly wonderful couple, learning something more about partnership or timing or trust. As we waltz, we depend heavily on one another, on the local church body, and on the saints who have gone before us.

The local church body is God's ordained means of protecting and sustaining us as we waltz through life. When we live life in community, preaching the gospel to ourselves and one another, serving one another and allowing ourselves to be served, and "[being] filled with the Spirit, addressing one another psalms and hymns and spiritual songs, singing and making melody to the Lord with all [our] heart[s], giving thanks always and for everything to God the Father in the name of our Lord Jesus Christ, submitting to one another out of reverence for Christ,"—well, then we are fulfilling God's glorious intentions for the local church body (Eph. 5:18–21).

But it is not just our local and contemporary church brothers and sisters who make up the fellowship of God. As believers we stand on the shoulders of the people of God who have loved God long before us. This view will give us a more full vision of what we are to experience in heaven, when people of all tribes and tongues and *through all eras of the church* will finally be together worshiping God in one accord. We are well-served now to check our beliefs and our doctrines against those church fathers and mothers who walked the journey of faith before our time. We can check both our arrogance and our individualism by seeing if we really believe what the historic church has taught.

The local church body is God's ordained means of protecting and sustaining us as we waltz through life.

And not if, but when we find ourselves out of line and perhaps leaning toward individualism in one way or another, it is simply another invitation back to the Gospel Waltz. If we are waltzing, the fruit of humility is going to be evident because as we have seen: repentance breeds humility. And humility breeds repentance. Humility in a community setting is unstoppable because it is simply an invitation to more and more and MORE community. Those who have experienced life change as a result of surrendering to Christ's invitation to dance will create a culture of safety because they will create a culture where people are not afraid to repent. And guess what? People who see others repenting are likely to also feel safe doing the same. And so the cycle goes. More and more people are invited to waltz with Jesus because of the influence of those around them who are also waltzing with Jesus.

The Fruit of a Waltzing Life

As we live, we see that there are certain seasons of life where we are putting out a whole bunch of fires, and it can feel like life is out of control. It can even feel like it is all on us—whatever the "it" of that season might mean. Inevitably, our stress level goes sky high, and it can feel like the enemy is winning.

When you waltz for many years you will find that repetitive behavior leads to a growth of muscle memory. Just as athletes talk about muscle memory in swinging a golf club or putting a spin on a tennis ball, the more we waltz the more it will become a part of our spiritual muscle memory. By grace, now when I enter an especially out-of-control season of life, I view my rising emotions as a check engine light. And by grace, over time we can begin to catch ourselves more and more. Every time it is an invitation to enter the waltz, to ask God and our hearts where we are being invited to repent, how we are being asked to remember the gospel, and where we are being invited to be shaped in Christlikeness. It is about making the connection between the overwhelming or discouraging circumstances and the music of God's pursuit. By grace, more and more when I see the check engine light flare on, the first thing that enters my mind is *God this is your pursuit of my heart. How can I respond to this pursuit by pursuing you back?*

And that is what the fruit of a waltzing life looks like: receiving Christ's invitation to dance and participating with the music, the ballroom, and, most importantly, the Partner.

But what are some more specific areas of growth we can expect to see as the fruit of a waltzing lifestyle? We can expect humility, peace, and increasing affinity for the disciplines of the Christian life.

Humility is a natural outpouring of one who continually practices a lifestyle of repentance and faith. The more we repent, the more we will see our need for repentance, as God's holiness is revealed to us in ever-increasing portions. We begin to realize that all we have and all we are is all grace. And that is humbling.

Peace is the natural response for those who begin to embrace all of life as God's pursuit of our hearts. Those who trust that the symphony is all under the control of the Good Conductor will not fret when they hear the startling thunder of an unexpected kettle drum. They will not believe it has just ruined a beautiful violin adagio, but instead they will be curious as to how God is going to invite us to waltz through this next movement.

And finally, we see an *increasing affinity for the spiritual disciplines* of the Christian life—things such as prayer, reading Scripture, attending worship, participating in community. Our understanding of these disciplines moves from seeing them as a transaction of grace (where I get because I give) to viewing them as a means of grace (where I pursue from a place of love and desire and need). Rather than thinking we are loved or blessed (or not loved or blessed) because of our level of engagement with spiritual activities, we begin to embrace them as a way to return our gratitude and love to the God who is constantly in pursuit of us. We begin to see them as a means to help us pursue him right back because we love and long to do so.

Numbers 21 and The Rest of the Story

In Titus 2:14 Paul highlights the difference between the want-to and the ought-to when he says that part of the purpose of Christ was to "purify for himself a people for his own possession who are zealous for good works." Grace changes the disciplines from have-to to want-to. But make no mistake, we are not lifeless sticks floating down the current of the river toward godliness. D.A. Carson, one of my seminary professors said, "People do not drift toward holiness. Apart from grace-driven effort people do not gravitate toward godliness."[27] Because of the fall, left to our own devices we will drift toward one of the twin ditches: self-effort or complacency.

We see this drifting when we follow to completion the story of the bronze serpent from Numbers 21.

[27] D. A. Carson, "For the Love of God," https://www.thegospelcoalition.org/blogs/justin-taylor/sanctified-terms-for-our-drifts-from-holiness/.

Nearly 1000 years later the serpent-turned-relic is still around, this time being adored by the Israelites as a good luck charm and even worshiped as an idol.

Their hearts had drifted.

In their midst, during the days of the Divided Kingdom, King Hezekiah was known as one of the "good guys"—one of several good kings of Judah, the nation of the South. While the Northern Kingdom of Israel was being conquered by the Assyrian Empire and Hezekiah's own father was leading Judah deeper and deeper into idolatry, Hezekiah "did what was right in the eyes of the LORD" (2 Kings 18:3). King Hezekiah removed local shrines of false worship, destroyed idols, and even "broke in pieces the bronze serpent that Moses had made" (v. 4). It would seem that in the midst of Judah's idolatry, the Old Testament church had adopted a magical understanding of the bronze serpent, allowing the object to take on power apart from that of God.

The church's infatuation with the object—this symbol (or anything similar, really)—reveals the danger of worshiping signs instead of the thing it signified. Just as with baptism or the Lord's Supper, it is not the elements or signs that are to be worshiped, but the One who is signified, Jesus.

Our hearts can turn even good things into idols, because just like the Israelites our hearts are always looking for something to worship besides Jesus. Even the bronze serpent, this symbol of mercy and salvation, ended with the people mis-appropriating the promise, believing the power was in the metal snake and not in the God who used it as a shadow of a far greater redemption. Their idolatry was a call back to step one, back to repentance, and to a renewed belief in the supremacy of the One they were called to obey.

The destruction of the serpent at the hands of Hezekiah was a call for Israel to waltz all over again.

There is a tale (which may be more myth than fact) that the Polish pianist Jan Paderewski was scheduled to perform at a great concert hall one evening at a high society, black-tie extravaganza. Present in the audience was a mother with her fidgety nine-year-old son. As the mother turned to talk to some friends, the boy, tired of sitting in his seat, slipped away found himself strangely drawn to the black grand piano on stage. Without much notice from the sophisticated audience, the boy climbed the stage steps, sat down at the stool, stared wide-eyed at the black and white keys, and placed his small fingers in the right locations as he began to play "Twinkle, Twinkle, Little Star."

The pre-concert crowd roar hushed as hundreds of frowning faces turned in the direction of the stage and then began to shout that someone should get that kid off of there. Backstage, Paderewski overheard the sounds out front and quickly discerned what was happening. Without one word of announcement, he walked up behind the little boy, reached around both sides of his shoulders and began to improvise a beautiful counter-melody to harmonize and enhance the boy's tune. As the two played together, Paderewski kept quietly speaking over the boy's shoulder where only he could hear, "Keep going. Don't quit. Keep playing."

It is the very same with the Gospel Waltz. We will never be finished until Christ returns or calls us home. We continue to be the boy that knows so little of the spiritual life that in our immaturity all we can play is, "Twinkle, Twinkle." But our teacher is the Master, and he takes our childish steps and leads us in the continuous 1, 2, 3 of the Christian life. Sometimes we waltz with him in a fluid manner and sometimes haltingly, but we never stop. We do not "arrive" and we will not "finally get it." We simply 1, 2, 3, Repent, Believe, Fight . . . and then begin again, all the while standing on our Father's feet, reminded that he is the one who has been leading all along.

Chapter 8 Summary

- Waltzing doesn't fix us; it's simply how broken Christians in a broken world live broken lives, all the while experiencing substantial life change until Christ returns or calls us home.
- Waltzing is a continuous, lifelong process.
- Waltzing can help us understand and engage with our ongoing sanctification.

Reflection Questions

1. Engage with the statement, "I don't want to just know that I'm loved. I want to be changed by that love."
2. Are you involved in a church community that actively motivates your heart, spirit, and actions toward a lifestyle of repenting, believing, and fighting? If not, what might it take to seek out such a community? If so, what kind of participant in that community do you want to be?
3. Consider the fruits of a Waltzing lifestyle: humility, peace, and increasing affinity for the spiritual disciplines. In which area have you recently experienced the Lord grow you? Which stands out as the area where you'd most like to experience growth?
4. Are you currently living a Waltzing lifestyle?

9

WALTZING ON DIFFERENT DANCE FLOORS

The waltz is nothing if it is not applied.

In the following chapter you will find what I intend to be practical examples of true life application. Please do not begin this book here, as my prayer is that you would engage with the content of the previous chapters so that your heart is ready for what could otherwise read as a performance checklist or, heaven forbid, as a checklist for God's approval.

But make no mistake, Jesus purchased our growth in holiness (1 Cor. 1:30) and not merely our deliverance from hell. By pursuing our hearts through the variations of Waltz music, he asks us to dance in the form of circumstances, relationships, and life. He is making us aware of our sin, guiding us through repentance, re-establishing our belief, and bringing us to a place of delighted obedience. It is fully in God's providence (that is, his kind sovereignty over the lives of believers) that he is bringing circumstances into our lives to expose bondages to sin that would not have been exposed had those providences not put us in these certain circumstances.

I submit to you that all that is happening in your life—all the pleasure as well as the pain—is happening because God is orchestrating circumstances and relationships to open your eyes to his presence so that you might experience progressive, spiritual freedom as you abide with Jesus—as you waltz (Job 23:10; James 1:2–4; 1 Pet. 1:6–7). The fundamental truth is this: God is at work around us all the time. He is always pursuing our hearts in love and always showing us our need for Jesus.

It is this kind providence that is, after all, seeking to bring about our spiritual freedom. Just as with the Israelites, God cares most about our hearts' devotion to him. Apart from those providences putting you and me into our specific tight circumstances, our bondages would never have been exposed. God is orchestrating circumstances to lead you and me to repentance—to lead you and me to begin to waltz—*so that* we might experience more of the amazing and transforming grace that God is showering upon us. We must continually be reminded that it is God's kindness that leads us to repentance (Rom. 2:4).

All that is happening in your life is happening because God is orchestrating circumstances and relationships to open your eyes to his presence, so that you might experience progressive, spiritual freedom as you abide with Jesus—as you waltz.

The following are some specific areas where God may be inviting you to waltz.

In Personal Life

Our perspective about our circumstances will change when we see God as the One bubbling things up to the surface in our response to struggles so that we can experience the beauty of Christ's redeeming love and power in fresh ways.

One night as I was walking out the door to speak at a Bible Study (which was all about grace and holiness and living in repentance) Laurie said, "I hope you're going to be home early tonight." I looked at her and said, "Well, we'll see."

Now, when she asked me that, I knew very well that I was not going to be home early at all. I had already planned on playing in a basketball game with some friends after the Bible study. I did not want to tell her what it was that I was going to do because then she might try to talk me out of it, and I might not get my own way. So I was just sort of nice and polite and said, "We'll see," when in fact I was deceiving my wife (while on my way to teach about grace and holiness and living in repentance).

I wish I could say that I walked back in the door and repented right then and there. I did talk to her about it and even repented of not telling her the whole truth. But sadly, it was not until after I had returned home from playing basketball that my heart was softened to see the truth of what really went on in our interaction.

God's commands have three main purposes:

1. To expose our sin and show us our need for Christ (Rom. 3:20; Rom. 7:7; Gal. 3:24)
2. To lead us to fresh repentance and faith (Gal. 3:19, 22)
3. To show us the good, acceptable, and perfect ways of life (Rom. 12:2)

In the first purpose, we view God's law as a tutor or even a teacher who will show us our sin and take our hand to lead us to Jesus. As we engage with Scripture across any number of topics, we allow this first use of the law to lovingly expose us and show us our fresh need for Christ.

In the second and third purposes, God's commands and prohibitions in Scripture are given to lovingly reveal God's will more clearly to our regenerate hearts, which will be renewed in repentance and faith. God's commands reveal to us what love for him looks like and what love for our neighbor looks like. This is our Fight step, where we engage our renewed wills to make godly choices.

You have heard it said, "If you aim at nothing, you'll hit it every time." Well, it holds true for godliness as well. We are to grow in holiness day by day as we bring our hearts to the Word of God. The Word of God then exposes where we need to repent. And then we do so particularly and specifically.

In the instance with my wife, first I repented before the Lord as he exposed my finagling about the basketball game and seeking my own interests above hers. I entered (briefly) into the Believe step, preaching the gospel of grace all over again to my own heart. And then I moved toward an actionable step—fighting for our relationship and our marriage by repenting specifically to my wife.

I offer this specific instance as a model of sorts. As we look into some of the dance floors of life we will see that circumstances and details may differ, but what remains the same is the heart behind the forward motion of the Gospel Waltz.

In our personal thought lives we have many opportunities to waltz as our sin is exposed. If you are looking to invite the Holy Spirit to reveal sin so that you can enter into the waltz in regard to thought life, you may find questions like the following helpful:

- What have the majority of my thoughts been about today?
- Are there any thought patterns I have willfully chased after today that I would be embarrassed if they were made public?
- How has my tongue led me astray today?
- What has my tongue revealed about my heart (Matt. 12:34; James 3:2–12)?
- Have I manipulated any conversations to control the outcome or cast myself in a beneficial light?
- How have I finessed my own weaknesses or failures so that I do not appear as bad as I really might be?
- Have I held back from sharing the whole truth with myself or others?

In Personal Prayer Life

Our prayer lives are a barometer of our spiritual lives. We can diagnose how much we are really gripped by grace and how much we really believe the gospel by allowing ourselves an honest assessment of our prayer life. Prayer is not what good Christians do; it is what desperate Christians do. It is how we waltz.

Choose any Christian virtue you are being called to grow in. For example: self-control. Say to yourself upon waking up, "I'm going to be self-controlled today" and take note of how quickly that mentality lets you down. That is just not the way the gospel works. Rather, when we say,

> "God, show me where I'm lacking self-control so that I can bring my sin to Christ and trust in the transforming power of the cross in my life and

> then, by the Spirit, dependently fight for self-control"—now THAT is fertile ground for change.

I just waltzed very quickly through a Christian virtue that is lacking in my sinful heart. I invite you to practice with your own struggles on this framework. Note that this does not have to be some huge, drawn-out process where the steps take days or hours or even minutes. Recognizing I have sinned against the Lord is an invitation to waltz every single time—including quickly in my own head.

When we waltz, we are praying smarter, not harder. Prayer does not have to be a difficult means of grace. I firmly believe further incorporating the practice of the Gospel Waltz into our existing prayer life will help us all grow and be stretched.

> "Ugh, Lord, I've done 'it' again. Please forgive me. I am not forsaken because of (this particular sin) Jesus. Guide my steps."

or

> "Oh Father, I can't seem to stop lashing out at those around me! Forgive me, God. Thank you for Jesus's perfect speech, his perfection on my behalf. Change me, God!"

Two seconds of heart-felt prayer, and I have waltzed. I am assured that I am experiencing the supernatural power of Christ (1 John 1:9).

Or perhaps:

> "Lord, I just exaggerated my goodness and minimized my sinfulness. I did that because at that moment my righteousness in Christ meant noth-

ing to me and I wanted to establish my own record of righteousness. Forgive me and empower me to rest in my alien righteousness so that I will be more honest and vulnerable."

or

"Lord, I was just so critical and self-righteous toward my friend/my spouse/my child. The fact is that I have sinned similarly just a short time ago. Lord, it's amazing how I want grace for myself but want to use the strict measure of the law for others. Help me to see my own sin and experience your grace as a result and then enable me to express that same grace toward others."

We can sometimes hear the music of God's pursuit of us in *how* we pray. Sometimes we pray more like orphans than sons and daughters. Let's think through the Orphan Waltz again. First, I experience the music of God's pursuit through my own brokenness. As a result of hearing the music in this way I feel threatened, so I defend myself. I disbelieve the gospel and my identity in Christ so I believe I must measure up by my own record of righteousness. Since my only ground of confidence in the orphan mentality is myself, I am overwhelmed with fear and doubt. So I try harder and find my sin is again exposed. But since I am still believing it is all up to me, I am not free to acknowledge or grieve my failure. As a result, I again rationalize my sin. Defend. Disbelieve. Do. Defend. Disbelieve. Do. My prayers in this case would be focused on stopping the music instead of focusing on repentance and dependence on Jesus to change me more than my circumstances. An orphan prayer would focus on God fixing things. The music of God's pursuit is not primarily about a change in circumstances but a change in our hearts.

In Personal Study of God's Word

Certainly God pursues our hearts in the waltz music we hear through relationships and circumstances, but we must always remember that Scripture is the most pure type of waltz music. When we read the Bible devotionally, memorize Scripture, hear sermons preached or engage in small group discipleship, the Scriptures are wooing us to the Father, inviting us to dance.

We can respond appropriately to this wooing by taking care not to read Scripture and immediately think of ways we need to "get busy," but rather to examine our hearts for ways the passage is exposing our fallenness and sin. I hope that does not feel depressing to you. I assure you it is anything but! Our joy comes from seeing Christ as our Savior and Deliverer and experiencing his love and power, and that happens when Scripture reveals our sin and points us back to our hope in Christ.

A word on effort: many people approach the Bible with an assumption or presumption that the stream of consciousness running through their minds is God. But that approach is incredibly dangerous because our family of origin, our brokenness, our strengths and weaknesses, and even our personality all impact how we read Scripture. The voice of God can only be known through the proper interpretation of God's Word. And yes, that requires effort, study, commitment, submission of our own will to God's will, and assenting to the work of the Holy Spirit to be our guide. This is why prayer and Scripture reading have to hold hands.

When someone mines for gold, they are often digging in darkness for weeks, months, or even years, hoping to find a nugget. They use a variety of tools, endless patience, and persistence—even when there is not clear progress. It takes great study and hard work to read Scripture accurately, and we need to think critically as to whether the impressions we have as we read are God revealing himself to us, or us imprinting our views on God's Word.

In truth, this practice is likely more difficult than most of us in the church have been led to believe. Now I am not saying everyone needs to have a seminary degree. What I am saying is that having an accurate interpretation of Scripture and wisely choosing which pastor, Bible study leader, or friend we study the Bible alongside is vital. God's Word is life, and our handling of it in study, devotion, and teaching should reflect the esteem we give it.

As we study Scripture, the three waltz steps are on nearly every page. To practice finding them, we can learn to ask questions of every text we are reading and begin waltzing.

Repent

Is the Spirit exposing a heart attitude through the text that I need to repent of?

Is the Spirit exposing a wrong behavior through the passage that I must confess?

Is there something wrong that I have thought, said, or done that is revealed in the text?

Is there something that I have left unsaid or undone that is revealed by the passage?

Is there an area of unbelief that is being pointed out by the Spirit as I read?

Is there a heart-change and/or life-change God is calling me to make that I am resisting?

Is there a "fruit" sin exposed that is leading me to acknowledge a "root" sin in life?

All life change begins with repentance, but it does not stop there. It leads to the second step of the waltz: Believe. So as we read Scripture we can ask:

Believe

Is there some element of the work of Christ that I have been resistant to believe?

Is there a "present value" of the blood of Christ that I must apply to my heart?

Is there a promise of God that I need to appropriate?

Is there a revelation of grace that I need to relish?

Is God's love expressed to me in a fresh way that I need to rest in?

Is there a goodness, kindness, or mercy of God that I need to thank him for?

Is there a revelation of the law as my highest delight that I need to embrace?

Is there a prohibition that I need to acknowledge as a warning?

As the Believe step leads to a fresh experience of the message of grace as supernatural, transforming power, we experience that power anew, and only then are we called to step out in fresh faith and new obedience, trusting in the blood of Christ to empower us.

So then we come to the Fight step.

Fight

After appropriating the power of the blood, is there a command I need to obey?

After appropriating the power of the blood, is there a prohibition I need to heed?

Is there a means of grace I need to engage in?

Is there a ministry activity that I need to carry out?

Is there an act of love or mercy that I need to follow through on?

Is there a temptation that I need to struggle hard against to overcome?

Is there a battle with the world, the flesh, or the devil I need to take more seriously?

Is there something revealed about my life for which I need to be held accountable?

Additionally, the fruits of the Spirit offer a memorable and accessible spiritual exercise in applying the Gospel Waltz. Each week we can choose one fruit to focus on: love, joy, peace, patience, kindness, goodness, faithfulness, gentleness, or self-control. For instance, if we focus on gentleness we would ask

God to make us aware of where we are not being gentle toward others. In interactions with others the Spirit might make you or I aware of the lack, which we can then repent of. Then, affirming our justified standing and adopted status, we would trust in the power of the Spirit to be activated in our life in specific regard to gentleness. We can trust that God delights to hear us ask him for this fruit in our lives. Finally, we can step out into our day with new confidence in the power of grace to inspire and enable gentleness. As we realize afresh how gentle God is with us in our lack of gentleness, it will soften our hearts and compel us toward bearing this fruit in increasing degree.

In Missional Living

The gospel is for you, but it is not all about you. I'm thankful for my good friend and chairman of Mission to the World, Lloyd Kim, for making this distinctive connection between the Gospel Waltz and missional living through evangelism and discipleship. Part of our progressive transformation toward intimacy with Christ is seeing God develop a heart for those who don't have a personal relationship with him, whether they be the neighbors next door or the nations overseas. It's quite common to begin to engage in the Waltz from the starting point of our personal relationship with Christ. But it must not stop there. The Holy Spirit was given to us to pour out God's love in our hearts (Rom. 5), to bear fruit in our lives (Eph. 5:18) and to empower us for witness (Acts 1:8). The last thing Jesus said before his ascension into heaven is found in Matthew 28:18–20, "And Jesus came and said to them, 'All authority in heaven and on earth has been given to me. Go therefore and make disciples of all nations, baptizing them in the name of the Father and of the Son and of the Holy Spirit, teaching them to observe all that I have commanded you. And behold, I am with you always, to the end of the age.'"

Most believers know rationally that we are called to share our faith and to be engaged in bringing the gospel to the nations (Pray! Give! Go!). Sadly, few followers of Christ have ever personally led anyone to Christ, been on a short-term mission trip, or given sacrificially to the cause of global evangelization. Our gospel witness is not only about offering everyone that breathes the opportunity to hear the good news and receive eternal life. Witness is also about the glory of God being proclaimed and the name of Christ being honored.

As we waltz with Christ, we need to embrace our responsibility to invite people who don't know him into the dance. We are not merely called to enjoy dancing with Jesus, we are called to go out to the highways and byways to compel others to enter the ballroom. We are called to witness in both word and deed. As we waltz with Jesus toward greater transformation, our lives bear an aroma that captures the attention of others. And the more we waltz, the more effective witnesses we become to the world; the more we shine as stars in the darkness (Dan. 12:3; Phil. 2:15). But our deeds alone in living a holy lifestyle won't lead others to faith in Christ. The message of the gospel must be on our lips.

All heart transformation begins with repentance. We can repent over our tendency to be self-absorbed even as believers, and repent of giving in to the temptation to think the Christian life is just about our intimacy with Jesus or our individual spirituality. Next, we preach the gospel to ourselves, rehearsing the story of our need and God's abundance again and again. It should come as no surprise that our need to practice pressing belief deep down into our hearts serves to ready us for opportunities God presents to us to share him with unbelievers. The more we experience grace the more likely we are to express grace to others.

Finally, we can engage in moving toward effectively sharing our faith with others. We can receive training in outreach or make use of the many available tools which will keep the nations before our hearts and minds on a daily basis. We can give regularly to global missions and sign up for a short-term mission trip. We can even read the daily news or watch newscasts and read and listen with missional eyes.

The more we experience grace the more likely we are to express grace to others.

The aim of the Waltz is not merely progressive sanctification. While waltzing leads to great transformation in our own hearts in this life and moves us toward evangelism and mission, neither are the end goals of waltzing: the glory of God is. May God be honored by our holy lives and by our holy witness.

In Response to Outside Stressors

There is one element of life that often brings us to the point of acting the fool, and it is that needling four-letter word—*pain*. Pain can cause many Christians who under normal circumstances are regularly abiding, worshiping, and joining in Christian community to do exactly the opposite. It can lead them to relatively disappear—just like an orphan. If you remember the Orphan Waltz, each waltz step is distorted to try to stop the music and keep us from moving to the next step because we cannot even complete the one we are on. Suffering often kicks Christians who are otherwise chugging along into this orphan mentality. When our aim is waltzing continually and abiding in Christ rather than relief from trials, we can help fight back against this orphan mentality and dance intimately with Jesus through whatever music he is ordaining in our lives, even in response to pain.

As we examine the hurt we are experiencing, so often what we are after is relief. We will do anything that holds out hope to have that suffering numbed, even if just for a moment. It is difficult to keep at the forefront of our thoughts that just as in the story of Joseph, when our stories are flooded with pain, evil means it for harm but God ordains it for good (Gen. 50). This is not to minimize the sorrow over the pain we experience. As a matter of fact, God reveals that he can even weep over that which he ordains. Think of the death of Lazarus. God ordained that death for his glory, for the good of the kingdom, and for redemptive purposes in the lives of Mary, Martha, Lazarus, and others. Yet Jesus still wept (John 11). Jesus never fails to be a sympathetic High Priest for his people. At the same time, he is always at work around us to use pain to bring about our ultimate redemption. As we waltz, we can begin to view our suffering as transformational.

I have seen firsthand how trials can be both heart-wrenching and transforming in ways that bring much glory to God. There are a myriad of ways pain can transform us for good, but one way I hear most often is of the intimacy people feel with the Lord during personal devotional time. In trying times, our devotions take on a fresh invitation into the divine dance with

Christ. It is as if during a time of suffering Scripture and God become so intimate that we experience them as they always should be. We are absolutely desperate and gutted to our core, and Jesus is still everything he ever said he would be: near and enough. In those moments, his words are the only balm our souls can take.

In General Relationship

Whether it is the difficult co-worker, the strained relationship, a challenging roommate, an untrustworthy boss, an unsupportive in-law—we all have those relationships that God brings into our lives that seem to expose our sin over and over again.

When it comes to challenging relationships, it is easy for us to look through the normal end of the telescope when we are looking at someone else's life and magnify their sin while minimizing our own by looking through the wrong end of the telescope at ourselves. By grace, God wants us to turn the telescope around and recognize that the portion of their sin we are witnessing is dwarfed by the amount of sin we are aware of in our own life. We also need to acknowledge that their sin is God's issue to deal with in his timing and not our issue or responsibility. God will take care of that person according to his will and way. Moreover, when we turn the telescope the right way, we see our own sin in far more adequate light—a light that will hopefully guide us to the first step, repentance.

In all sorts of relationships, repentance breeds repentance. A broken heart leads to other broken hearts, and the best way to develop humble relationships is not through pointing out everybody else's sin, but exposing our own. And as we are broken over our sin, it is likely to cause other people to weep over their sin.

My friend John told me about a committee meeting he attended once where each person was asked to share the authentic state of their heart, but no one seemed to be going very deep or addressing real issues or real sin. When it came to be John's turn he felt a little hesitant, but decided to go for it. He shared deeply about the pain in his life related to being a dad of adult children. He shared in such a way that those in the room could see who he really was and how he was struggling in the moment. Thankfully, not only did those in the room respond appropriately in a way that made him feel seen and known, but the rest of the individuals who shared after him did so from an entirely different place than those who had come before. John's authenticity bred authenticity, his repentance bred more repentance, and his humility bred love.

In Marriage

Of all three of the bents of heavy-footedness, the two most common are the heavy-footed repenters and the heavy-footed fighters. I imagine you will not find it too surprising to learn that these sin bents often find one another and decide to unite together in marriage. I would like to tell you about three marriage counseling situations I often am invited to speak into.

First, there is the common occurrence of one spouse being a workaholic. As they watch the shrapnel of their workaholic bomb detonating, they see the impact on their marriage, their kids, and even their own quality of life—and they feel bad about it *all the time*. Every time they are in Bible study that is what they are confessing. They feel guilt and shame, and then they feel ashamed about what they feel shame over, but nothing is changing because all they are doing is feeling bad about their workaholism. They are stuck in remorse, and while they may be trying to engage the Gospel Waltz, they are stuck in the Repent step—if indeed it even is true repentance. They carry so much weight of remorse and heavy-footed repenting that all they see is their own failure. When all you see is your own failure, you are likely to become depressed about it, and you are likely to lose any motivation to keep going. You can become an Eeyore.

The other spouse, in this instance, commonly picks up all the slack of the home life, working his or herself to the bone to make sure the kids are taken care of, the house is looked after, and the day-in/day-out functions of the household click along at the best possible pace. Sure, things are running, but this often leads to a detached spouse whose resentment level is rising each day and whose respect toward their mate is diminishing because they are barely giving the time of day.

This hamster wheel the workaholic spouse finds themselves on will certainly not lead to the Believe step. They may be trying so hard to change, but there is no Jesus in the trying. Belief is completely absent. They are confessing all the time but not engaging with their spouse over the hope of the gospel and how it propels us toward godly living, joyful relationship, and the courage to make hard life changes when necessary. What is missing in the workaholic spouse's continual confession and repentance is the hope of Christ. Because only casting ourselves completely on Jesus's completed work will lead to real transformation.

The second pattern I see in marriage counseling situations is people who are so focused on the other person's sin that they see the other as the bigger sinner. Therefore, they lack the ability to see their need to repent of their own sin. What follows is that they are often filled with self-righteousness, they are clueless as to how big their own sin is, and they are unable to show patience or compassion toward their spouse. Instead, they are judgmental, and all the while spite, disdain, anger, apathy, or indifference are building. As these attributes grow, the self-righteous spouse starts to despise the other.

A third common pattern is that of women who are strong in the Fight step, committed to the actionable steps of an outward Christian walk, but whose husbands are more passive. She does all the right things. She reads her Bible, memorizes Scripture, participates in Bible study regularly, and even goes to counseling. While the husband may go to church and be involved in discipleship, she is constantly criticizing him for not being godly enough or spiritual enough because in her eyes he is not "doing enough." Over time, the husband, beaten down from her attacks, loses his will to engage even to the degree he is currently involved in.

The tragic irony is the wife's focus on her husband's sin has completely blinded her to seeing her own. She has pushed him to the point where he feels like he cannot do anything right in her eyes, so why try? Meanwhile all the wheel-spinning in chasing after acts of love and service and study do not seem to be changing her heart all that much either. She is struggling with all kinds of idolatry that she is not able to deal with because she is caught in a loop of thinking that if she just goes to one more Bible study, attends one more counseling session, or reads one more spiritual growth book then she will finally be living the spiritual life.

I am amazed at how many distorted ideas there are about marriage and about what it means for the man to be the spiritual leader in his home. There is a bunch of goofy stuff out there. Men, if you really want to know what it means to be the spiritual leader in your home, be the chief repenter. If you set the pace in repentance, you will be the spiritual leader. Do you want a woman who is in love with you and is impassioned by your walk with Christ? Then be the chief repenter in your home. What draws a wife to Christ is not a husband who seems to have his act together. What draws a wife to Christ and to her husband's heart is seeing his brokenness and neediness for Christ. That is the simplicity of spiritual leadership.

As we saw in the personal prayer life section of this chapter, our prayer lives act as a barometer of our spiritual health. When it comes to our married lives, our prayer lives may likewise indicate our spiritual health, but it may be more helpful to examine our *thought lives.*

When it comes to marriage, an orphan waltzer may find themselves thinking:

> *I'm so frustrated about my wife's nit-picking. She's driving me nuts.*
>
> *If only he would help out around here. He doesn't even see what needs to be done in the house.*
>
> *Well, if she's going to act like that then I'm just not going to even engage. She needs some counseling.*

He doesn't care about me. He only wants me around to pick up after him.

In prayer or in thought life, the orphan waltzer will first defend themselves, taking the focus off of their personal sin and putting it on what is wrong outside of themselves. Instead of bringing the troublesome instance or pattern before the Lord, they are thinking or praying about the person or the circumstance. They are left feeling alone, abandoned, and as if whatever needs to happen in life, marriage, housework, or child-rearing is all up to them.

The Orphan Waltz thinks the aim is to stop the music. The Gospel Waltz says you need to let the music lead you to change.

But someone who is practicing the Gospel Waltz will think and pray differently:

Oh, I am irritated. God, help me see how I'm contributing to this rough patch. I know you are in control, and I know you want my marriage to be a satisfying one. I am totally dependent on you to give me the resources to engage with this difficult circumstance.

I know I can drive her nuts too. God, give me kindness in how I respond to her right now. You are always kind to me. Show me how to extend that to her.

The Orphan Waltz thinks the aim is to stop the music. The Gospel Waltz says you need to let the music lead you to change. Every note of every circumstance is orchestrated by a kind and loving God who is inviting you to dance with him through them. Everything he sends into our lives is his pursuit of our hearts. Each circumstance is set in such a way as to reveal our brokenness, expose our idols, and show us our greater need for Christ, who is drawn to us as we experience brokenheartedness and will apply the supernatural power of the gospel to transform us. We have developed a Gospel Waltz vs. Orphan Waltz template for the Gospel Waltz Journey Retreats we offer, which can help you think through how it looks to face God's pursuit as an orphan compared to as a son or daughter. See the appendix for this template.

Whether you find yourself in these generalized relational examples or not, I hope you will see what is of far greater importance: the invitation to waltz.

In Parenting

Leading in Repentance

As important as it is to train up our children in the Lord, it is just as important to realize that God is using our parenting experiences to train us up in the Lord. God is always pursuing our hearts in a redemptive fashion through every situation and circumstance we face with our children. We often act as if what is going on is all about our children, and clearly to some extent it is. But what if we stopped to remember that God is pursuing our hearts through it all? What if we remembered that what is happening is just as much about us and our response?

Being the chief repenter also applies to parenting. In parenting (as in marriage), I find we have some oddball ideas and expectations about what it should look like and how we should act. I have no doubt that one of the best things we can do for our kids is to repent in front of them.

By doing so, we can kick-start their understanding of what it looks like to abide in Christ and to live out the Christian faith. When we model repentance, we allow them to see us entering in at the most natural starting point of the Gospel Waltz. And then we model how we preach the gospel to ourselves, believing that the Lord has not stopped singing over us, remembering that the Christian life is supernatural and change begins by the power of grace, and modeling how we may need to take an action step toward reconciliation. Outside of physically or emotionally abusing our children, perhaps the most damaging thing we can do to them is to pretend to have our act together. We will end up raising little Pharisees. By grace, may our pattern be that we show them that repentance is the norm for the Christian life.

When my co-author Holly and one of her friends were talking about repenting before their children, Holly asked her friend if she thought we could go overboard in repenting to our children, making them wonder if we really didn't have it together at all.

"What's the alternative?" wisely replied the friend.

Clearly, what we repent of and who we repent before requires discernment and maturity, but in general, there is not enough vulnerability or transparency in our homes and churches.

Leading in Emotional Safety

I grew up in a context where the message I caught was "it's not okay to be sad." Whenever I would feel troubled by something, the message I received from adults was to toughen up because when the going gets tough, the tough get going. Just like in the Pixar movie *Inside Out*, Joy was always trying to keep the controls from Sadness because she thought Sadness could only ruin things. It was not until I saw the movie that I realized I had done that with my own children, and it grieved me.

I realized that whenever my children were anxious, fearful, or sad, I was doing the same thing that was done with me without intending to. I was trying to fix them rather than hearing their hearts and affirming what they were experiencing. In effect, I was being dismissive of their feelings. What they needed was not for me to fix them, but rather for me to hear them and tell them it was okay to feel what they were feeling. That was my opportunity to help them see their need for Christ in the brokenness of this world and in their own fallenness. But I skipped over it by trying to take them directly to the Fight step. A counselor in our church body, Emily Walker, says that what remains hidden will be multiplied. After watching *Inside Out*, I now believe that what remains unknown will be multiplied, and it grieves me to realize that is what I have done in parenting my children. But even now, I can rest that God was still at work in spite of my brokenness, even using it to transform my children into the parents they would one day become. Still, I pray that my repentance over that oversight will be redeemed by the Father's kindness, and that I will be transformed into being able to hear the hearts of others when they share difficult emotions with me.

Leading by Being Parented Ourselves

My friends Tim and Laura Bennett adopted a little girl—their fifth child—from an orphanage in China at the age of 6. Of the difficult days dealing with separation anxiety on their arrival in the United States, Tim recounts:

In the ensuing weeks I would come home from work and sit in my chair, and she would come sit in my lap and just look at me. She would say, "You Daddy," and I would say, "Yes, I'm Daddy." Then she would say, "I Caelyn." And I would say, "Yes, you're Caelyn." And she would ask, "Daddy love Caelyn?" I would smile and say, "Yes, Daddy loves Caelyn!" She would follow up with, "Mommy love Caelyn?" and I would say, "Yes, Mommy loves Caelyn." Then she would repeat her question with each of our children's names as if she expected the answer might be different at some point. Once everyone was enumerated, she would smile the biggest smile, jump down and start playing. But, in just an hour's time, she would get back in my lap again and repeat the same exact sequence of questions.

In her first few weeks with us, she did this four or five times a day. I would put her to bed and say prayers, and she would look at me with a smile and say, "Daddy love Caelyn?" There were times when I wanted to shout, "Yes! Daddy loves Caelyn! Mommy loves Caelyn! All God's children love Caelyn!" But I knew a deep transformation was taking place. You could see in her eyes: Caelyn was grappling with the concepts of *love*, *family*, and *father* for the first time in her life.

One of the things Caelyn received when she left the orphanage was a small photo album with pictures of her and her friends in various activities and settings at the orphanage. In those first few weeks, we spent many hours looking through the photo album with her, as she would try to describe her friends and where she had lived. When my parents came to visit her for the first time from North Carolina, my mom was thoughtful enough to bring her own photo album with pictures of our extended family to show Caelyn. As they were sitting on the couch, I saw Caelyn point to a picture and say, "Bennett?" My mom said, "Yes, that's Bennett!" And Caelyn's eyes got big. After a few minutes, she jumped down and ran to get her photo album from China. I thought she was going to also share pictures with my mom, but I couldn't have predicted what would come next.

Caelyn pointed to a picture in my mom's photo album and said, "Bennett?" And, when my mom said, "Yes, that's Bennett!" Caelyn peeled back the protective covering in my mom's album and took out the picture. Then, she opened her photo album, took out a picture from the orphanage and put it aside, replacing the picture from her album with the photo from my mom's album. By the time they had finished, Caelyn had emptied half the pictures from my mom's photo album, and pictures from the orphanage in China were strewn all over the couch. As I began to process the significance of what I had just witnessed, I realized Caelyn was opening herself up to the depths of love and family. She was surrendering her old identity and basking in her new identity.

When we believe that we are loved so deeply that Zephaniah 3:17 is *always* true of us—that the Lord is with us, rejoicing in us, quieting us with his love, and singing over us without ceasing—then we can embrace the heart that Caelyn embraced and see ourselves as a part of God's family, parented continually by his loving-kindness. This belief is so transformational that it will impact every single part of our lives, not the least of which is our parenting. And when we are truly gripped by this belief, by grace we will be enabled to pass it along to those God has called us to parent.

In Friendship

How do we, as the people of God, look out for one another?

The gospel of grace leads us to safety in being honest and authentic in friendship. When the gospel of grace exercises real change in us, we find that we no longer need to uphold appearances. We do not have to exhaust ourselves trying to put off the vibe that we have it all together. The first point of the gospel is that we do not have anything together—we are actually worse off than we ever realized. And no matter how hard we might want to try to make other people think we have it together, we know no one does. So instead of wasting time sitting around wondering what is wrong with each other, we might as well begin to tell each other. We really know when the gospel of grace is changing our lives because when we are boasting so completely in Christ and our identity in Christ, then we will be the first person to risk it and say, "Look, here's who I am." Does this mean there is no place for discernment? Absolutely not. Do we hang our dirty laundry everywhere in front of everyone? Of course not. Does it mean that we never do anything right? Thankfully, no.

However, an unrepentant lifestyle is the norm of the world, therefore the more we are in the world, the easier it is to think that an unrepentant heart is the norm. The reverse is true with gospel friendships: the more we draw near in friendship to those who are living a waltzing lifestyle, the more we will realize (and act on!) the waltz as the norm.

Sadly, I have witnessed many friendships simply end rather than seek to work through a disagreement, a perceived slight, or an actual slight. But when we are committed to a gospel friendship, we have a far better option than just walking away. We have the invitation and opportunity to grow in grace and sanctification (and to invite our friend to do the same) by engaging with the Gospel Waltz.

Not *if,* but *when* you are the source of wrongdoing in a friendship, repent! First, go to the Lord and seek his forgiveness. Then repent to your friend and seek reconciliation with them. This does not have to be some big production—just a simple, "I am so sorry I engaged in gossip there, will you please forgive me?" Then engage in the Believe step by reminding your heart of the good news of the gospel that no one has it all together, and ask God to pour out the present, transforming power of the blood of Christ at the place of repentance and to move in you to take steps to become a better and more trustworthy friend.

If we are the one who has been wronged in a friendship, we are called to forgive as Christ has forgiven us. As we walk in repentance over our own sin on a daily basis, we experience God's love and forgiveness. Those who regularly experience God's forgiveness are most likely to express it to others.

When things are a little less straightforward, my friend and fellow pastor Gary Purdy has a helpful phrase he recommends to use in awkward friendship situations. When we find ourselves in a sticky friendship situation and we do not know the who's, what's, and when's of what's going on, a helpful tool is to just say, "This feels weird" to our friend. In a true gospel friendship, this will serve as an opening for authentic conversation about the wrong, an airing of grievances if necessary, and then a move toward repentance and reconciliation.

In Engaging with the Commands of God

When it comes to the gospel, we encounter both gospel privileges and gospel responsibilities. In Paul's letters, the gospel privileges always appear first, setting the basis for the gospel responsibilities. This is why engaging with the Fight Step is so critical: the Holy Spirit clearly teaches through Paul's letters that there are an abundance of commands that reveal what a Christ-centered life looks like. The call to obey is never legalism if we are clear that our obedience flows *from* acceptance and is not *for* acceptance. Throughout Paul's letters we read commands related to sexual purity, avoiding divisiveness, promoting the purity of the church, avoiding overindulgence, taking care of family, controlling our anger, submitting to government institutions, paying taxes, serving the world, being sensitive to weaker Christians, not judging other Christians on gray areas, controlling our words, pursuing humility, and fighting against fear—just to name a few. All of these commands fill the latter portions of every letter Paul wrote. These imperative sections are waltz music. The commands of God reveal our sin and call us to repentance. The commands of God show us a fresh need for transforming grace and remind us that the Christian life is not just difficult, but impossible apart from the power of the Holy Spirit. Then, finally, the commands of God point us to the aim of the work of the Spirit in our lives. The commands of God reveal what Christlikeness looks like and what love for God and love for neighbor look like.

With respect to obedience and holiness in the Gospels, some Christians have noticed that compared with the same in Paul's letters, though there is no tension, there at times is a difference of emphasis. Paul's commands often relate to what many call "Christian ethics." It is what most evangelicals think of when they think of holiness. However, the Gospels speak just as much about Christian ethics and holiness, but at times with a different emphasis. When we listen to Jesus and his gospel ethic, it often has to do with remembering the poor, giving water to the thirsty, food to the hungry, clothes to the naked, comfort to the sick, dying, and imprisoned (Matt. 25:31–46). Jesus focused on the condition of the heart and the attitudes within as much or more than he taught on behaviors. He taught often about having a heart of love, kindness, mercy, reconciliation, compassion, humility, and servanthood. Jesus clearly spoke on the self-righteousness and legalism of the Pharisees that lurks in all of us as well. Whether we look to the words of Paul or the words of Jesus, all the commands of God are the music of our Father's loving pursuit of our hearts; his words are the waltz music that leads us in the rhythm of Repent, Believe, Fight.

In Stewardship

Jesus taught more on money and possessions than he talked about faith or prayer. Have you ever wondered why? Because few things expose our hearts like finances. Jesus says where your treasure is, there your heart will be also. Generosity is never really a finance issue; it is first a *love issue* and therefore a *heart issue* and therefore a *gospel issue*.

The car breaks down, the kids need braces, the air conditioning in the house goes out and the bills from the vacation come due. All at once. Coincidence?

Or, is God at work around us all the time, pursuing our hearts in love, exposing our need for the Savior with waltz music so that we would experience his transforming love and power in fresh ways?

We often talk about worship, prayer, reading the Bible, and communion as means of grace—and they are—but how often do we talk about financial stewardship and tithing as a means of grace? Waltzing is what leads us more deeply into the heart of Christ. Waltzing leads us more completely into conformity to Christ. Our heart toward money, possessions, and generosity will be exposed through waltz music constantly. This area provides wonderful opportunities for life change.

We are also called to practice good stewardship with the unique expression of our gifts, skills, and abilities. Jesus told parables that emphasize our need to fight for faithfulness in stewardship. In Matthew 25:14–30 we read of the parable of the talents. Three servants were given talents by the master according to their ability. Two of the servants did business and doubled what was entrusted to them. The third servant buried his talent and did not make any effort to make a profit. We must seek to be faithful workers in the kingdom of God. This does not mean that to be faithful, all need to go into full-time vocational ministry. What it does mean is that each of us must recognize that all our gifts, skills, and abilities must be maximized for the flourishing of the world to the glory of God (Jer. 29:5–7). Remember, the Scriptures provide waltz music in 9.1-channel surround sound. When it comes to the gifts, skills, abilities, and talents you have, are you regularly acknowledging them as gifts from God? Are you surrendering them to his use and his glory and for the flourishing of the world? Or do you see them as *your* skills that *you* have developed for *your* own use and *your* own profit and benefit and comfort? You see that there can be lots of fodder for repentance in this area.

So let's say we're exposed. What do we do? We boast in the gospel by preaching the gospel to ourselves and reminding ourselves of our unchangeable identity in Christ. Then, at the place of our repentance we appropriate the present value of the blood to change our hearts and transform our minds, emotions, desires, and choices. Finally, equipped with the confident assurance that we are filled afresh and empowered by the Holy Spirit, we seek to attack life with new purpose, new direction, new motives, and new aims.

Much the same can be said about the stewardship of our time. In Ephesians 5:15–16 Paul commands us to be careful about how we live, "not as unwise but as wise, making the best use of the time, because the days are evil." Paul is saying that we must buy up all the time from evil use and redeem it, restore it, and put it to the very best use. Elsewhere he tells us to do this because the time is very short and must be budgeted on all kinds of accounts. We give time to relationships (friends, spouses, children), to vocation (whether inside or outside the home), to spiritual activities (worship, studies, mentoring, service, mission), and to hobbies, exercise, eating, drinking, and sleeping. We often speak of planning a budget for money. But how often do we look as rigorously at our use of time? Are we as intentional with our time as we need to be? The reason for such questions is not to produce shame and guilt. We are secure in Christ. We have the anesthetic of grace in our lives so that the scalpel of God's commands are not fearful to us. We can love God's law because it points us to all that is beautiful and good and true. We ask these hard questions because they are the music of God's loving pursuit of our souls. Unless we see our brokenness and sin we will not be changed. So we get honest and look for areas where we need to repent, which leads us to a fresh need for Jesus and his grace. And as we learn to drink more deeply of Christ through the gospel promises, over time we will be changed in our thoughts, feelings, desires, and choices.

In Vocation

We spend much of our waking lives in the pursuit of our vocation. Vocation has at its root the idea of calling. As we would believe, that is a calling from God. Yet many Christians struggle to connect God to their work.

My lovely bride breeds Golden Retrievers, and I am continually encouraged and challenged by how she connects her vocation to God and his kingdom. When she considers which dogs to breed for a new litter of pups, she weighs their strengths and weaknesses as well as their lineages. As a thoughtful breeder, she is tasked not just with providing wonderful dogs as new family members, but also working toward improving the breed overall. I love the kingdom-oriented and redemptive aim of that perspective. She is improving the breed. She is making things *better*. She is working to turn back death and brokenness.

I believe my wife's application of kingdom work is a view we would all benefit from aiming for in our vocations. I hope we would all work in such a way that we strive to bring beauty and glory more clearly into the world, and not just for the sake of chasing after a paycheck. Work is not a necessary evil; it is a pre-Fall institution. We will work into eternity in the New Jerusalem. Vocation is one of the greatest ways the kingdom comes on earth as it is in heaven—whether our vocation be running a household, running a law firm, running after weeks-old puppies, or running a corporation. As Martin Luther said,

> The prince should think: Christ has served me and made everything to follow him; therefore, I should also serve my neighbor, protect him and everything that belongs to him. That is why God has given me this office, and I have it that I might serve him. That would be a good prince and ruler. When a prince sees his neighbor oppressed, he should think: That concerns me! I must protect and shield my neighbor. . . . The same is true for shoemaker, tailor, scribe, or reader. If he is a Christian tailor, he will say: I make these clothes because God has bidden me do so, so that I can earn a living, so that I can help and serve my neighbor. When a Christian does not serve the other, God is not present; that is not Christian living.[28]

In other words, the Christian cobbler does his duty not by putting little crosses on the shoes, but by making good shoes, because God is interested in good craftsmanship.

God is at work all the time at your place of work, pursuing your heart in love. Each and every work frustration you encounter is just a different variation of waltz music playing as God's invitation to bring change to your heart. If we were to actually believe that, we

[28] Martin Luther, "Sermon in the Castle Church at Weimar," October 25, 1522.

would find far different attitudes at work toward assignments, relationships, difficulties, successes, frustrations—*everything.* With this view, each and every component of our work life would be shrouded in God's sovereignty and providential care of us, his children.

At work it can be especially complicated to recognize and repent of our heavy-footedness because we may come to realize that our heavy-footed bent toward the Fight step just feels normal. Our heavy-footedness may even seem to benefit us while at work! On the surface level, striving for acceptance, purpose, and success can reap short-term benefits, but whether it is in work life or spiritual life, this posture is sure to reap disastrous long-term consequences.

As I have shared, one of my consequences is that I fall into a try harder mentality all the time, and I can seek to live independently of Christ. As I am preparing to preach I still struggle with the temptation that what is most necessary for sermons to be powerful is my study, my scholarship, and my constant editing. Now, I know better! I know only God is going to change lives, but the way I work so hard betrays a paradigm that it is really my preparation that is going to change lives.

I am constantly repenting of self-effort. I find this subtlety extremely difficult, and it requires my constant attention. Because of course I want to do the best I can, be prepared, do good exegesis, have good transitions, and share memorable illustrations. But before I know it, I am trusting in those things instead of walking into the pulpit saying, "God, unless you show up this isn't going to change anybody."

For you it may not be preaching, but it is no less true of any other vocation. It may even be easier to find danger in your vocation if you struggle to think Jesus is not involved (for instance, "Jesus isn't going to make this sale, I am! Jesus isn't going to replace that heart valve, I am. Jesus isn't going to fix this leaky toilet, I am"). If you are finding your paradigm exposed right now, repent! What a beautiful place to be invited to waltz with Jesus.

Now What?

I often ask the people I mentor to answer a few questions related to the Christian life. What is your understanding of the Spirit-filled life? How do you know if you are filled with the Holy Spirit? What does it mean to abide in Christ? How do you know if you are abiding in Christ right now? Their answers often relate to observable evidences of the Spirit-filled life or abiding in Christ. They often mention the fruit of the Spirit: love, joy, peace, patience, kindness, goodness, gentleness, and self-control. Sometimes their answers are purely subjective. For instance, "I know I'm filled with the Spirit if I am experiencing calm or happiness." If I ask a few more questions, people start to feel insecure fairly quickly: How do you know if you are experiencing the kind of calm or happiness that is due to being Spirit-filled versus being just circumstantial? Do you think it is possible to be filled with the Spirit and yet lack any subjective experience that you in fact are? Do you think it's possible to not be filled with the Spirit yet subjectively be convinced that you are?

There is a lot of confusion among believers surrounding the Spirit-filled life or abiding in Christ. Yet a good case can be made that these are critical elements to the daily lives of Christ-followers. What I have attempted to offer in these pages is simply a tool that might help all of us understand and live out the supernatural life in the Spirit. I have tried to put feet to the gospel by presenting abiding in Christ as a three-step dance with Christ through which the Triune God turns our mourning into dancing. When Paul tells us in Ephesians 5:18 to be continually filled (directed and empowered) by the Holy Spirit, quite simply he is reminding us of the call of Christ upon our lives to keep on repenting (Mark 1:15), believing (Mark 1:15), following (Mark 1:17), and fighting (1 Tim. 6:12). Each one of the steps of the Gospel Waltz is essential and critical. There is no waltz without all three steps, and there is no Spirit-filled life nor any abiding in Christ without all three steps.

In any real-life dance you have the elements: the music, the dance floor, and the steps of the dance you choose to follow. The same elements are present in the Gospel Waltz. The music is the situation or circumstances orchestrated by God's loving pursuit of our hearts to show us our need for Christ and to draw us closer to him. It is what ultimately moves us to take the first step of our dance. The dance floor is the setting of life where the opportunity to dance arises. The steps of the Gospel Waltz are our response to the music of God's pursuit—Repent, Believe, Fight. The purpose of the Gospel Waltz is not a way to stop the music nor to get off the dance floor. The purpose is to help us stay engaged with what God is doing in our lives as we respond to his love. We continually learn how desperately we need Jesus to change us, we see how God supernaturally turns our mourning into

The purpose of the Gospel Waltz is to help us stay engaged with what God is doing in our lives as we respond to his love.

dancing, and we grow in the satisfaction that we are bringing glory to God.

The beauty of the Gospel Waltz is that it avoids overcomplicating grace. It keeps us away from the ditch of self-righteousness and self-reliance on the one side and the ditch of self-indulgence on the other. The power of the Gospel Waltz is that it leads to a regular experience of the supernatural, transforming, present value of the blood of Christ for our daily lives. The humility of the Gospel Waltz is that it reminds us that though we are genuinely new, we are not yet completely new. We will wrestle with the pull of the flesh until the day we die, and we will always need to be invited back into the dance. The practicality of the Gospel Waltz is that it applies to every arena of life. The Dance Floors upon which we are called to waltz with Jesus are many: Friendships, marriage, parenting, vocation, spiritual disciplines, decision-making, finances, temptation, suffering, pain. In every arena of life, the Triune God is pursuing our hearts in love to draw us into deeper intimacy. God orchestrates the music (circumstances and situations) that ends up exposing our sin and our desperate need for Jesus, which in turn leads to gospel transformation as we Repent, Believe, and Fight. The longevity of the Gospel Waltz is that we dance until we go to be with the Lord. Waltzing does not fix us. It is simply how broken people with broken lives live in a broken world until Christ returns, yet all the while experience substantial healing, growth and transformation. The Christian life involves groaning inwardly and waiting expectantly (Rom. 8:18–30). As my friend Scotty Smith once shared with me: "What does a hope-filled, Spirit-led, gospel-saturated Christian life "feel" like? Less like a relaxing massage at a spa and more like the pain of childbirth, with the guarantee we will be TOTALLY like Jesus."

In essence, the Gospel Waltz is allowing ourselves to be pulled in close to Jesus so that we experience more of the reality of our union with him. It is embracing the Christian life, which is by grace from first to last; it is never moving beyond this grace, but always moving more and more deeply into it. So, as you engage in this dance, may you continually feel the love of the Savior pulling you in close as he leads you in the Gospel Waltz. May you experience more of your need for Jesus, more of your identity in Christ, more of the transforming power of the gospel, and more of the exciting adventure of living full-on and full-out for him.

POSTFACE

When Bob asked me if I would be interested in working on this Waltz book together, my immediate reaction was enthusiasm. As a proponent of enthusiasm, a book person, and a long-term congregant of his church, I recognized how rare it is for one from Bob's flock to be able to guide him in return. Not many of us are granted the opportunity to serve the one who has so faithfully preached grace and gospel to us week after week. But I didn't get to savor the invitation long before it turned to gripping fear.

I voiced my concerns to a friend, "If we're really going to get to work together, what happens when I disappoint him or frustrate him or annoy him?"

"Isn't it obvious?" she replied.

My brow furrowed. "No," I quietly admitted.

Ever the gentler one in our friendship, she said in the least judgmental way possible, "Holly, you waltz."

Oh right.

Got it.

I tell this story to underscore not just my own need, but also what is perhaps my favorite of the Waltz applications: we waltz in community. *Always and only.* In isolation we are weak. Left to our own devices we are forgetful, authors of irrational narratives, or worst-case orphan scenario-constructors. Alone we don't (and can't!) grasp the Father's abundant love and pursuit of us in and through our circumstances. But we are not supposed to live the Christian life alone. We are intended to do so in community, where when our vision gets blurry we can benefit from the safety of the clarity of gospel brothers and sisters.

If we are engaging in the Gospel Waltz, then we are doing so in community. And in the mercy of that ballroom we are never alone. Yes, we are in the arms of Christ, but even more so as we lift our eyes from his gaze and glance around we see a myriad of others of all ages, nationalities, degrees of sanctification, and generations of the church throughout time. We see our sisters and brothers in Christ—the communion of saints throughout all generations—and *they too are dancing.* Each is waltzing with Jesus, and each is urging us to do the same.

These friends alongside us in our modern lives, these are the friends who are tasked to remind us, to point around the ballroom and say in the gentlest way possible, *Look where you are! Remember who's holding you! You can do it—take the next step. That's it, lean more on your partner. Hey, that move you just did there—that was cool! I want to try that one myself . . .*

The gospel ballroom is filled with the enthusiasm of the communion of saints cheering one another on.

Bob, I am cheering you on as you enter this next phase in a career of faithfulness. Thank you for your steadfastness in preaching grace and gospel to me and my family for many, many years. Thank you for being the voice in my head urging me on in my own pursuit of Jesus. And thank you for the invitation to join you on this book journey. It's been an honor. What's next?

Holly Mackle
November 2022

Appendix A:
Gospel Waltz Overview

The Orphan's Creed	**The Beloved's Creed**
I am in control of my own destiny.	*I have a God who is in control.*
I am on my own.	*I am a beloved child of God.*
I need to work extremely hard for acceptance.	*I am justified by faith in Christ.*
No one out there has my best interests at heart.	*I am sanctified by faith in Christ.*
I am the only person I can trust.	*I still deal with indwelling sin.*
I cannot let anyone see my weaknesses.	*I have a loving Father who pursues me.*
If it's to be it's up to me.	*My life in Christ is supernatural.*

Exposure (Music)

What is the presenting issue or circumstance?

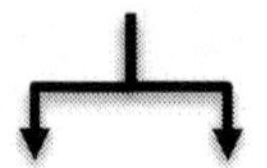

Orphan Waltz	**Gospel Waltz**

Defend	***Repent***
How am I tempted to respond in this situation?	*How is my sing exposed in my tempted response to the Music?*

Disbelieve	***Believe***
What am I tempted to believe in this situation? (About Myself, God, and Others)	*In light of the gospel, what is TRUE about this situation? How does the gospel empower me to live out these truths?*

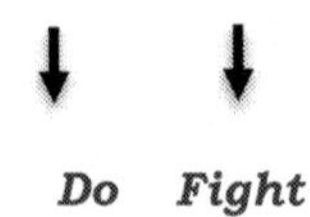

Do	***Fight***
If what I'm tempted to believe is true, what are my options?	*What does the gospel engaged fighting back look like in this situation?*

Appendix B:
Journaling the Gospel Waltz

Orphan Waltz *vs.* Gospel Waltz	
The Dance Floor	
The Music (the situation)	
What are my initial feelings in this situation?	

Orphan Waltz	**Gospel Waltz**
On the surface, what am I wanting in this situation?	*At a deeper level, what am I longing for in this situation?*
Defend *How am I tempted to respond in this situation?*	**Repent** *How is sin exposed in my tempted response to the music?*

Disbelieve	**Believe**
What lies am I tempted to believe or truths tempted to disbelieve in this situation? (About myself, God and others.)	*What gospel truths is God calling me to affirm in this situation? How does the gospel empower me to live out these truths?*
Do	**Fight**
If what I'm tempted to believe is true, what are my options? *How would I pray?*	*What does gospel-enabled fighting look like in this situation?* *How would I pray?*

Acknowledgements

During my doctoral studies, Dr. Donald Guthrie was a constant encourager of my DMin dissertation, which ultimately gave birth to this book, and Dr. Philip Douglass told me at my Dissertation Defense that I had to write a book on my conclusions. Thank you, Donald and Phil, for your wisdom, counsel, and friendship. I owe a huge debt of gratitude to Dr. Bryan Chapell who was used, perhaps more than any other, to open my eyes to grace as the motivation and empowerment of all spiritual health and growth.

Another thank you is due to the Session of Oak Mountain Presbyterian Church for two sabbaticals, during which I first wrote my dissertation and then began the seed work of this book. I also extend my immense gratitude to the congregation of OMPC, which has responded to the concepts and doctrines presented here with a hunger and interest that most pastors could only dream of. In particular, I want to express my deepest appreciation to my "fellowship" of Ruling Elders, whose constant encouragement and spurring led to the completion of this project: Tim Bennett, John Lankford, Barry Morehead, and Tom Majors. We've walked many miles alongside one another, and by God's grace I pray we have many left in our pilgrimage together. Thank you to Tim Bennett, whose own processing of the gospel waltz in his life helped me make so much progress in this project and led to the creation of the Gospel Waltz Journey retreat and follow-through process. In addition, the "A-Team," my ministerial staff colleagues at OMPC, all played a significant role in the creation and refinement of this material.

As this project has been twenty-two years in the making, it has benefited from the input of many people. Among them are Greg Smith, Heather Parker, Lisa Donahue, Jennifer Geralds, Brian and Jennifer Phillips, Phil Chambers, Melany Guzzo, and Monte Starkes. My thanks to Julie Sparkman for her unique and constant encouragement. And to my two pastor cohorts: you guys have been great sounding boards and have contributed to my own walk with Christ in ways you'll never know.

To my friends in Northern Ireland who provided a home away from home: Stephen and Heather Williamson, Alistair and Angela Bill (and their daughter Sarah), and Gary and Christine Burnett—thank you. I also am especially grateful for my dear friends Mark and Anne Goudy, who encouraged me in spreading the waltz to Northern Ireland and invited me to Coleraine Presbytery to bring the waltz to the Presbyterian Church of Ireland.

My administrative assistant at OMPC, Rhonda Blevins, has helped both me and this project in so many ways through the years. Thanks to Beth Meadows for transcribing scores of sermons from which many lines in these paragraphs arose. Thank you, Kayla Neely, for your very able graphic design work.

Cara Johnson, I felt you were in my head at times as I worked on how to communicate the Gospel Waltz more effectively. You were a champion of the grace of God and a bulldog in your desire to see truth communicated effectively in these pages.

I can honestly say that were it not for my dear sister and partner in this project, Holly Mackle, my writer, this book would never have come to fruition. Holly, you are an absolute joy to work with. You believed in this book from the start, you were encouraging throughout the process, and you were even willing (sometimes too willing?) to critique my thoughts and words. You weaved together countless conversations and years of sermon material in a masterful way, and you made this book better than I ever could have on my own. Well done.

I am grateful to Jeremy Writebol, Lauren Bowerman, Lainee Oliver, Benjamin Vrbicek and the rest of the wonderful team at Gospel-Centered Discipleship who championed this book. Thank you for believing the Gospel Waltz can change lives beyond the walls of my local church.

To my children, Josh, Hannah, and Michael: I remember asking you often if being a pastor's kid was good or hard. Your answers were almost always that it was a good thing. You'll never know how that filled my heart with joy and fueled my faith. I hope you saw your dad waltzing with Jesus as you grew up in our home. I pray that your children—of whom I am the proudest "BaBa" (Harmony, Own, Nora, Nolan, and Carter)—and your children's children's children will be waltzing with Jesus their whole lives long.

To my parents: I never cease to be amazed at the sacrifices you made from the very beginning. I have always felt loved by the two of you. And to my dear mother-in-law, Legare: your encouragement throughout the years has been nothing short of amazing. Thanks dear sis, Sue, for reading the draft and being so affirming.

And to Laurie. What can I say? I learned to Waltz *from* you. I learned to Waltz side-by-side *with* you. Your authenticity draws me to Jesus. Your kindness leads me to repentance. Your tenderness at my repentance multiplies and beckons me to deeper repentance. You have preached the gospel to my soul more than any other person on earth. You believed in the power of grace before I had a clue. As Phil Collins sings in our song: "Wouldn't you agree? Baby, you and me got a groovy kind of love."

Finally, I want to thank my Lord and Savior Jesus Christ. You have been so patient with me, as it has taken me decades since that profession of faith in the Pi Kappa Alpha House at Penn State in January of 1980 to be gripped by the gospel of grace. I know waltzing with you won't fix me this side of eternity, but it will lead to substantial growth and health. Thank you for purchasing my place in heaven for all eternity and for enabling my transformation in the here and now.

Other Resources

à Kempis, Thomas. *Of the Imitation of Christ*. Springdale, PA: Whitaker House, 1981.

Alexander, Archibald. *Thoughts on Religious Experience*. Carlisle, PA: Banner of Truth Trust, 1967. Reprint, 1989.

Alexander, D.L., ed. *Christian Spirituality*. Downers Grove, IL: InterVarsity Press, 1988.

Augustine, Saint. *The Augustine Catechism: The Enchiridion on Faith, Hope and Love*. Translated by Bruce Harbert. Hyde Park, NY: New City Press, 1999.

Bahnsen, Greg L., Walter Kaiser, Douglass Moo, Wayne Strickland, and William VanGemeren. *Five Views on Law and Gospel*. Grand Rapids, MI: Zondervan, 1996.

Bridges, Jerry. *Transforming Grace*. Colorado Springs, CO: Navpress, 1991.

Bruce, A.B. *The Training of the Twelve*, 4th ed. A.C. Armstrong and Son, 1894. Reprint, Grand Rapids, MI: Kregel, 1971.

Calvin, John. *The Institutes of the Christian Religion*. Edited by John T. McNeill. Translated by Ford Lewis Battles. Philadelphia: The Westminster Press, 1960.

Chamblain, J. Knox. *Paul and the Self.* Grand Rapids, MI: Baker, 1993.

Chapell, Bryan. *Christ-Centered Preaching.* Grand Rapids, MI: Baker, 1994.

———. *Holiness by Grace*

Coleman, Robert E. *The Master Plan of Evangelism.* Old Tappan, NJ: Revell, 1963. Reprint, 1981.

Cosgrove, Francis M., Jr. *Essentials of Discipleship.* Colorado Springs, CO: Navpress, 1980.

Creswell, John W. *Research Design.* Thousand Oaks, CA: Sage Publications, 1994.

Daloz, Laurent. *Effective Teaching and Mentoring.* San Francisco: Jossey-Bass, 1986.

Daloz, Laurent, Cheryl Keen, James Keen, and Sharon Daloz Parks. *Common Fire.* Boston: Beacon Press, 1996.

Dieter, Melvin, Anthony Hoekema, Stanley Horton, J. Robertson McQuilkin, and

John Walvoord. *Five Views on Sanctification.* Grand Rapids, MI: Zondervan, 1987.

Fisher, Edward. *The Marrow of Modern Divinity.* With notes by Thomas Boston. Edmonton: Still Waters Revival, reprint 1991.

Ferguson, Sinclair. *Children of the Living God.* Carlisle, PA: Banner of Truth Trust, 1989.

———. *Devoted to God: Blueprints for Sanctification.*

Garber, Steven. *The Fabric of Faithfulness.* Downers

Grove, IL: InterVarsity Press, 1996.

Hadidian, Allen. *Discipleship.* Chicago: Moody Press, reprint 1987.

Hagopian, David G. *Back to Basics: Rediscovering the Richness of the Reformed Faith.* Phillipsburg, NJ: Presbyterian and Reformed Publishing Company, 1996.

Hanks, Billie, Jr., and William Shell, eds. *Discipleship.* Grand Rapids, MI: Zondervan, 1981.

Hesselink, I. John. *Calvin's First Catechism.* Louisville: Westminster John Knox Press, 1997.

Horton, Michael. *Putting Amazing Back into Grace.* Grand Rapids, MI: Baker, 1994.

Hull, Bill. *The Disciple Making Pastor.* Old Tappan, NJ: Revell, 1988.

———. *The Disciple Making Church.* Old Tappan, NJ: Revell, 1990.

Keller, Timothy. *School of Servant Leadership.* New York: by the author, 1998.

Kuhne, Gary. *The Dynamics of Discipleship Training.* Grand Rapids, MI: Zondervan, 1978.

Lake, Kirsopp. *The Apostolic Fathers. 2 vols.* Cambridge, MA: Harvard University Press, 1912. Reprint 1998.

Lovelace, Richard. *Dynamics of Spiritual Life.* Downers Grove, IL: InterVarsity Press, 1979.

Lundgaard, Kris. *The Enemy Within.* Philipsburg, NJ: Puritan and Reformed, 1998.

Luther, Martin. *The Large Catechism.* Translated by Robert Fischer. Philadelphia: Fortress Press, 1959.

Luther, Martin. *Commentary on Galatians.* Grand Rapids, MI: Fleming H. Revell, 1924. Reprint 1988.

Manning, Brennan. *The Ragamuffin Gospel.* Portland, OR: Multnomah, revised 2000.

Miller, Jack. *Outgrowing the Ingrown Church.* Grand Rapids, MI: Zondervan, 1986.

Miller, Rose Marie. *From Fear To Freedom.* Wheaton, IL: Harold Shaw Publishers, 1994.

Moore, Waylon B. *Multiplying Disciples.* Colorado Springs, CO: Navpress, 1981.

Murray, John. *Principles of Conduct.* Grand Rapids, MI: Eerdmans, 1957. Reprint 1991.

———. *Redemption Accomplished and Applied.* Reprint. Grand Rapids, MI: Eerdmans, 1984.

Owen, John. *Sin and Temptation.* Minneapolis: Bethany House, 1996.

Packer, J.I. *Rediscovering Holiness.* Ann Arbor, MI: Servant Publishers, 1992.

Parks, Sharon Daloz. *Big Questions, Worthy Dreams.* San Francisco: Jossey-Bass, 2000.

Petersen, Jim. *Lifestyle Discipleship.* Colorado Springs, CO: Navpress, 1993.

Piper, John. *Future Grace.* Portland, OR: Multnomah, 1995.

Prior, Kenneth. *The Way of Holiness.* Downers Grove, IL: InterVarsity Press, 1982.

Rabey, Steve, and Lois Rabey, eds. *Side by Side.* Colorado Springs, CO: Navpress, 2000.

Ryle, J.C. *Holiness.* William Hunt and Company, 1883. Reprint, Grand Rapids, MI: Baker, 1981.

Spurgeon, C.H. *The Key to Holiness.* New Kensington, PA: Whitaker House, 1997.

Stanley, Paul and J. Robert Clinton. *Connecting.* Colorado Springs, CO: Navpress, 1992.

Swenson, Richard. *Margin.* Colorado Springs, CO: Navpress, 1992.

Tripp, Paul David. *Age of Opportunity.* Phillipsburg, NJ: Puritan and Reformed, 1997.

Tripp, Tedd. *Shepherding a Child's Heart.* Reprint. Wapwallopen, PA: Shepherd Press, 1995.

Wilhoit, James, and John Dettoni, eds. *Nurture That Is Christian.* Grand Rapids, MI: Baker, 1995.

Wilkins, Michael, J. *Following the Master.* Grand Rapids, MI: Zondervan, 1992.

Wilson, Carl. *With Christ in the School of Disciple Building.* Grand Rapids, MI: Zondervan, 1976.

Yancey, Philip. *What's So Amazing About Grace?* Grand Rapids, MI: Zondervan, 1997.

About the Authors

Bob Flayhart (DMin, Covenant Theological Seminary) has served as lead pastor of Oak Mountain Presbyterian Church in Birmingham, Alabama, for more than thirty-five years, and serves on the board of Covenant Theological Seminary. Bob and his wife, Laurie, have three children and five grandchildren.

Holly Mackle is the author of *Bright Star, The Story of Esther*, the family Advent devotionals *Little Hearts, Prepare Him Room* and *Connected Christmas*, and curator of the mom humor collaboration *Same Here, Sisterfriend: Mostly True Tales of Misadventures in Motherhood.* Holly and her realtor husband, David, wrangle two young girls in Birmingham, Alabama, where she is a lower school librarian.

About Gospel-Centered Discipleship

You may have noticed that there are a lot of resources available for theological education, church planting, and missional church, but not for discipleship. We noticed too, so we started Gospel-Centered Discipleship to address the need for reliable resources on a whole range of discipleship issues.

When we use the term "gospel-centered," we aren't trying to divide Christians into camps, but to promote a way of following Jesus that is centered on the gospel of grace. While all disciples of Jesus believe the gospel is central to Christianity, we often live as if religious rules or spiritual license actually form the center of discipleship.

Jesus calls us to displace those things and replace them with the gospel. We're meant to apply the benefits of the gospel to our lives every day, not to merely bank on them for a single instance of "being saved." A gospel-centered disciple returns to the gospel over and over again, to receive, apply, and spread God's forgiveness and grace into every aspect of life.

Resources from Gospel-Centered Discipleship

Visit GCDiscipleship.com/books.

"Develop your leaders . . . or die."

God doesn't want you to plant a church that "needs" its pastor all the time, a church where every answer to every question comes through the church planter. Instead, church planters must develop a community of leaders. *But how?* How do you develop leaders while preparing sermons, fundraising, and finding a new place to meet because you just learned your current meeting location got rented to someone else?

In *Primed to Plant*, seasoned church planter Dwight Bernier explores this topic and many other lessons he's learned the hard way. Whether you're just starting to consider the idea of church planting or whether you're already far enough along to know you need coaching, this book is for you.

Can't we all just get along?

Christians everywhere recognize the value of Holy Communion as a reminder of what Jesus has done. But author Timothy Shorey believes Jesus intends the meal to do *more* than simply remind. In these divisive and rancorous days—and as we see the Day of the Lord approaching—*The Communion Truce* helps us understand that participating in Communion is not for when every believer gets along and shares everything in common, but for when we don't—so that, by the power of the gospel, we can.

Does the reality of Heaven fill you with joy, dread, or boredom?

We all have thoughts and opinions about Heaven. But do they actually match what the Bible teaches? By asking and answering seven of the biggest questions about Heaven, Stephen Morefield guides readers through Scripture toward a surprisingly good, earthy, and compelling view of Heaven. Heaven is far greater than we think, and this book will set you to longing, always longing, for what comes next.

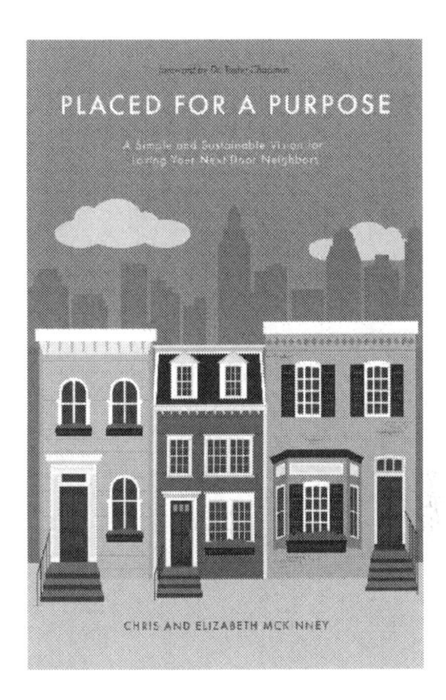

Many of us don't know our neighbors.

If we do know them, we aren't sure how to grow the relationship or talk about our faith with them. *Placed for a Purpose* provides a theologically rich framework for neighboring that helps people live missionally where God has placed them. Authors Chris and Elizabeth McKinney seek to provide a sustainable vision for the "low and slow" lifestyle of neighboring and supply practical tools that help people invest in their communities, value each step in the process, and build meaningful, gospel-motivated relationships with their fellow image-bearers right next door.

Your Next Step:
Take the Gospel Waltz Journey

Are you ready to take your journey to the next level and dive deeper into the transformational wisdom of The Gospel Waltz? If you are looking for an immersive, life-changing experience that complements and explores the book's teachings, look no further than The Gospel Waltz Journey.

What Is the Gospel Waltz Journey?

The Gospel Waltz Journey is a small-group-based, ten-week discipleship program designed to 1) embed you in deeply-authentic fellowship, 2) engage you in the truth of the Gospel, and 3) transform you through a personal application of the Gospel Waltz. Each Gospel Journey consists of:

- A three-day, immersive retreat to foster learning and team building.
- A ten-week follow-through process to apply the Gospel Waltz framework in the context of doing life together.

How To Get Involved

The Gospel Waltz Journey was created by GospelTree Ministries in partnership with the author.

If you are interested in bringing this resource to your community, visit www.gospeltreeministries.com/GWJ or if you would prefer to interact personally, you may contact Tim Bennett at tim@gospeltreeministries.com.

Made in the USA
Columbia, SC
24 September 2023